KUMAKAWA
MY TRUE STORY

Ross Hartshorn
&
Helen McCarthy

DEDICATION

In honour of Lord Theo,
my great mate and a true champion.

Here we are training together in our early days

ACKNOWLEDGEMENTS

Sending so much love and so many thanks to my very own special angel, Helen McCarthy, who helped me so much in writing my incredible story.

"Kumakawa is the most beautiful chestnut horse you could ever imagine. His great big white face shines with a loving and totally individual personality. However, the most attractive feature of this amazing animal is that to say the least, he is a bit of a rogue."

Ross Hartshorn

Looking smart as usual

INTRODUCTION

As you will appreciate from the photograph of me on the cover of this book, I am indeed a horse and, as I humbly like to think, a very handsome one. The title of this book includes my rather unusual name, Kumakawa, and this is the true story of my countless adventures in what I think is a brilliant life.

I will tell you how I got my name, all about my achievements (and under achievements) in horse racing and the amazing stories of my life. Then, following my 'alleged' retirement from the spotlight, I will tell you about all the escapades I have had during my incredible time as a pensioner. Living in the mountains of Wales, in the best home in the world with the most wonderful owner whom anyone could imagine. Helen McCarthy, a lady with the patience of a saint.

On many occasions, I will admit that have the tendency to be a very naughty boy - without doubt, I can be a creature of moods. The problem, with extremely talented individuals like myself, is that we can pick and choose when we want to perform, and this can be very frustrating for the loved ones who are close to us. With hindsight, I suppose I am a little disappointed that I didn't realise my full potential as a racehorse - because I know full well that, had I really put my mind to it, I could have won many more races. But, hey, life isn't all about winning and I know that I bring pleasure, exasperation and laughter to everyone around me.

During my racing days, and even now, my behaviour seems to depend on which side of the stable I get up on. I have definite likes and dislikes. I definitely don't like wearing a coat and I have taught myself how to remove one if fitted – much to the annoyance of stable staff. I never liked 'star jockeys' as they are too arrogant – so I wouldn't let them tell me what to do! Give me a nice inexperienced apprentice, and I would guide him or her all the way, whilst doing exactly as I liked, enjoying every second. As you might guess, I like to be the one in control.

Quirky – yes; moody – yes; naughty – yes. Special – VERY. Here is my true story – straight from the horse's mouth.

CHAPTER 1

NAMING RIGHTS & EARLY YEARS

I was born on 13th March 1998 to my mother Maria Cappuccini, who had a very brief relationship with my father Dancing Spree, one of those American tourists. This is the thing, Dancing Spree's father was the legendary Nijinsky, so that is why I am so gifted and so special. The fantabulous Nijinsky was my actual grandad for goodness, sake!

For the unenlightened, Nijinsky was a horse for whom there are simply no superlatives that come even close to describing his achievements. Although he was crowned Champion 2-year-old, unbeaten in five top class races in 1969, it was in 1970, as a 3-year-old, that he excelled. He became the first triple crown winner since 1935. Then, when winning the St Leger over a distance of 14 furlongs to give him his 11th straight victory, he was confirmed as one of the greatest flat horses of the century. I am proud to have a direct blood line connection to him!

The people who arranged the blind date between my parents were some financiers called Carlton Consultants and they were devilishly clever in coming up with my name. Grandad Nijinsky was named after the acclaimed Russian ballet dancer, Vaslav Nijinsky, whose virtuosity was, and still is, celebrated the world over. This in turn, by some clever deduction and word play, led to my dad being christened Dancing Spree. Often the naming of racehorses is an art in itself, with owners trying to link in something connecting the lineage. My family clearly had a 'dancing' thread entwined in the naming process already, Nijinsky being sired by the incredible stallion Northern Dancer.

Without doubt, one of those Carlton Consultants must have been heavily into ballet because, in 1998, the principal dancer at the Royal Ballet was Tetsuya Kumakawa, an illustrious Japanese ballet dancer who was only 26 years old at the time. How good must he have been then, at such a young age? The consultant made the incredible connection between the two outstandingly famous principal dancers and the name chain was extended.

So it was that I, already spotted as obvious star material, was given my name 'KUMAKAWA', affectionately to become 'KUMA' for short in future years. An hilarious offshoot of this often happened when I was racing, when it turned out that many racecourse commentators couldn't pronounce my name properly – the unlikely question often asked being "Is this horse, KUMAWAKA, Australian?"

.oOo.

After only a few short months with mum I left home and moved to Gainsborough, a lovely little market town in Lincolnshire. Here, in 1999, I was placed with a racehorse trainer just starting out on his own career. That trainer was James Given, a man who has gone on to earn a fantastic reputation within the sport of horseracing. James had to spend a fair bit of time showing me the ropes and teaching me all about racing craft while I was running fast. I really enjoyed all the hard work especially in such beautiful surroundings. At such a young age, I really enjoyed my free time in the paddock but there wasn't a great deal of play time, and I didn't get the opportunity to meet and bond with other horses in the way that I would have liked.

Nevertheless, I made great progress in my training, and I must say that I was very much looking forward to my first outing in a real race. Bright eyed and bushy tailed, on Friday 12th May 2000, I travelled all the way up to Carlisle for my very first competitive outing. This was my first experience of spending ages in a horsebox as it journeyed up the motorway, a travelling arrangement that was to become a way of life for me in the future. In fact, I quite enjoyed the travelling and, quite surprisingly I suppose, I never seemed to get bored.

Carlisle was a very long way to go for a first trip, however, and I gathered that James must have fancied my chances quite a bit. Yet, when we got there, I was really disappointed to discover that this race was a 5-

furlong sprint – a race that I thought was far too quick for me. Looking back at this first adventure though, some sort of alignment in the stars must have been occurring. I was drawn 13 and came in 13th – my lucky number - because I was born on Friday 13th.

After three more pretty ordinary runs for Mr Given, all over sprint distances that were far too sharp for me, I was sent to run in a selling race at Leicester. This race was over a mile, something I enjoyed and far more suitable for me - so I went to Leicester as a far more confident animal. This type of race typically involved horses of a lower class who had failed to make the grade. Their owners, quite simply, wanted shot of them.

I realised, of course, that this was a selling race, and the consequence was that I could in fact be bought and, therefore, be changing homes. Hiding my true feelings, I brazened it out and put it in my mind that, if the trainer wanted to move me on, I might be better off elsewhere. I had adapted pretty well to horsebox travel by now and it was with an extremely positive mindset that I went into this race determined to show exactly what I was all about. Over the mile it was so much easier for me to lay up with the pace and, with a furlong to go, I simply zoomed past the leaders to win without breaking a sweat. 25/1 was my starting price – a repeat of which was to happen quite a few times in the future. But, as per usual with me, trouble awaits.

A Stewards Enquiry was called to investigate my hugely improved performance. After my first four poor displays, the stewards thought that I wasn't much good. So how come I had won this race so easily? As with most stewards, they had no clue as to what I was all about and they didn't seem to reason that my previous races had all been far too short. Unsurprisingly then, Mr Given could offer no explanation at all as to why I was suddenly so good. After all, how could he possibly have known what I was thinking anyway or known what I was going to do?

Blank looks everywhere and that was, as they say, that. All the experts completely in the dark, I'll take that trophy, thank you.

Now that I had won, came the business end of the deal. I, Kumakawa, was to be sold at a racecourse auction. I wondered whether Mr Given would bid to keep me but he didn't. The bidding reached 4,500 guineas, at which point the hammer went down. I was sold to Mr Nilesh Unadkat, who turned out to be in partnership with General Sir Geoffrey Howlett - who, would you believe it, was the former Commander in Chief of Allied Forces Northern Europe.

I knew how honoured this man would feel to be taking on the grandson of the legendary Nijinsky and on 5th September 2000, I excitedly looked forward to finding out where my new home would be.

CHAPTER 2

INTRODUCTION TO
SOUTHWELL RACECOURSE

It transpired that my new owners placed me at a stable in Newark, Nottinghamshire, where I would be under the wing of trainer Mark Polglase. Southwell racecourse is barely 8 miles from Newark and this became almost my second home as I did all my training exercises there and a great deal of my actual racing as well.

Southwell was the only racecourse in the country which - in those days - ran on fibresand and this surface really seemed to suit me. (Recently, on the grapevine, I have heard that Southwell changed its surface to tapeta in summer 2021 – I wouldn't have been happy about that in my day.) Fibresand is a "very deep" surface to run on and it takes a lot of physical strength to get through it – a bit like running on loose dry sand at the beach.

Those initial days were happy times for me, and I enjoyed the environment of racecourse training and being with lots of different mates, although I didn't really make any close friends, something I sort of missed out on in these early years. On 20th October 2000 I had a nice warm-up race at Wolverhampton, a polytrack surface, where I came 3rd, before embarking on a very successful 3 race campaign at Southwell when I came 1st, 2nd and 1st. My sparkling form continued into 2001 and my handicap mark went shooting up to 85 (how good was I?) which meant that I would be carrying a lot more weight in my future races, which would also be of higher class.

I must say that it wasn't too long before all the relentless training around Southwell started to get to me a bit. Honestly, I didn't mind the hard work, but it was very monotonous, and I found it upsetting when Mr

Polglase decided to keep changing the distances I would run at. First of all, he changed me from running my usual 1-mile or 7-furlong trips to covering distances up to a mile and a half, but the last straw came when he entered me in a couple of 2-mile plus hurdle races at Huntingdon and Newbury. What on earth would grandad have thought? This scenario didn't sit well with me at all and in 2001 I became more and more discontented.

Unhappiness led to a mindset where my form plummeted and when, in January 2002, Mr Polglase entered me in another 2-mile hurdle race at Doncaster I got really fed up and quite unhappy with life. I must say that I wasn't very well motivated that day, trailing in 5th of 6 at 50/1 and beaten by 100 or so lengths, which is a very, very long way.

Then, on 14th March 2002, I discovered that my owners, after a conference with the trainer, had entered me into a claiming race at Southwell over my favourite distance of 1 mile. A claiming race is, theoretically, a lower standard affair than a normal handicap though not as poor as a seller, but such a race is often populated by good older horses or gifted troublemakers whose owners usually want to get rid of for a decent price. In a claiming race each horse has a price published in the race card and any animal, not just the winner, can be bought out of the race. Conversely, the allegedly lower-class race would give a horse the chance of gaining a win and, if the owners wished to oppose a claim to buy their horse, they could put in a "friendly claim" and lots would be drawn for the animal. If the owners kept the horse, they would have to pay the racecourse 10% of the claiming price as a premium. Paying to keep their own horse!

To be honest, I really did need another change of scenery and it was time to put my competitive hat on again. I couldn't be asked to keep jumping hurdles anymore and I knew that if I put my best foot forward, I could probably impress a prospective buyer, win or not. I knew it would be just potluck as to where I would end up but I sincerely believed that anywhere new was the best option. Sadly, this is a simple fact of life for so many of my contemporaries, I just hoped that I would be lucky.

.oOo.

Arriving at Southwell racecourse on that 14th March, I was absolutely delighted when I found out that I had been allotted a really inexperienced apprentice jockey to ride me. Now I knew that I could decide my own tactics and put my ability to full use. When a "so called" top jockey rode me everything usually went pear-shaped, probably because of my own belligerence but, put simply, I just know far more about what I am capable of than they do. Top jockeys never listened to instructions, always think they knew best and always refused to take even a second to learn how I could show my prowess in a race. That day I had Luke Fletcher on board. He was a 7lb claimer, right up my street, particularly on my favourite course and at my favourite trip. I certainly was not going to miss this opportunity to impress and took it with all four legs. Laying up with the pace for the first 6 furlongs, I swept to the front at the 2-furlong pole and stormed away to win by a huge 9 lengths.

Unquestionably someone would be interested in claiming me now, even though my advertised price of £6000 was not a bargain, particularly when 10% course fee and VAT were added on!

Sure enough, the trainer Damien Black put in a claim for me but so too did General Sir Geoffrey Howlett. I couldn't quite believe it, but my existing owners actually wanted to keep me. They must have thought a lot more of me than I realised. This meant that the two claims had to proceed to a ballot, a ballot which resulted in Damien Black taking me back to his stables. Damien had purchased me on behalf of my new owner Ross Hartshorn, who had as his partner the very special lady, Karen Graham. A lady who it turns out was also born on Friday 13th – my lucky number!

For me this turned out to be a relationship made in heaven and I loved them every bit as much as they loved me, and that must have been an awful lot considering the troubles we caused each other. The bottom line was that I always knew that this couple loved me just the way I was. Success or failure, they were always there for me, such a warm feeling to have. I always made sure that Karen held me when I was being saddled up, it gave me such a great sense of security.

Really surprisingly to me, as much as to everyone, after my stellar performance at Southwell, was the fact that, from then until the end May that year, I just couldn't get going at all. I was feeling very under the weather, so much so that when I was entered to run in a race at Wolverhampton in early June 2002, I really didn't fancy it at all.

I knew that Ross and Karen had travelled up to Wolverhampton overnight and had stayed in the hotel on course in order to be relaxed and all set to cheer me on. Nevertheless, on the morning of the race, when Damien came to take me out of the stable, ready to be loaded onto the horsebox, I really couldn't find the energy and, as I struggled to prevent the handlers extricating me from the stable, I caught the side of my face on the corner of the stable door and sustained a 12-inch cut right along the length of my jawbone. Now that really did hurt.

Not only did that mean that my trip to Wolverhampton was cancelled but it also gave me a nice 6-month break from racing which enabled me to have some really enjoyable rest and recuperation. At least Ross and Karen had a nice lunch that day and got home nice and early. Good job they seemed to love visiting me at the yard just as much as watching me racing. The bonus of this time off from the serious training was that I got the opportunity to get to know a few friends for a change. I was able to really make connections and firm friendships, not just brief acquaintances on the gallops.

Karen owned another horse at the yard, Hard to Catch - or "H" for short - and he was a multiple winner, something which he never failed to brag about. We got on like a house on fire and I am so grateful that during this period I actually learned how to build relationships with other horses, something that stands me in very good stead in these, my later years.

During my very happy years at Damien's yard, I enjoyed great friendships with other brilliant horses too, horses like Supreme Salutation, whom I became very close to when we were stabled together away from the main yard. Others included Beaufort, owned by Ross and Karen's great friends Ron and Milly Bright; Bucks, owned by the now famous trainer, Mike Murphy, whose fantastic yard I would pass through on my way to retirement; and the legendary Lord Theo, a super mate and a fabulous racehorse who won loads of races for Ross and Karen.

When I look back now, I realise, with true wonder, just how lucky I have been not only to have rubbed shoulders with these great horses but also to have had the privilege to call them my close friends.

Ross, Karen and my jockey Mark winning yet another trophy

CHAPTER 3

TROUBLE AHEAD

After a wonderful 6-months of care and pampering at the yard, with Ross and Karen visiting me every weekend without fail to make sure that I had lots of loving, I returned to full training and was put on the comeback trail. Damien had it in mind to target Southwell for my races, after all it was my favourite track, I loved the surroundings and really felt at home there. Following my long break, I needed a couple of warm up spins to get up to speed, so as to speak, and after that Damien decided to enter me for two separate races, both over a mile, at the track. These races were only two days apart, on 14th and 16th January 2003. In both races young Chris Cogan was "jocked up", he being an apprentice jockey claiming a 5lb allowance. The first race was a handicap race that my current low rating might prevent me from running in, while the one on the 16th was an apprentice claiming race which I thought was just a backup in case I didn't get in the handicap race. For sure I only expected to run in one of these races.

Everyone was delighted when I got into the handicap on the 14th and, not only that, I was the last one to qualify which meant that I would only be carrying 7st 13lb, bottom weight and my lowest ever racing weight. This raised my confidence to sky high levels, I felt really good and on top form and, if I say so myself, I ran an absolute blinder. 16/1, a big price as usual.

Chris held me up in midfield before, at the 3-furlong marker, he unleashed me with a withering run, cutting down the opposition one by one until, on the line, I was beaten by a short head (probably only a centimetre) by a horse called Kanz Wood -even though I whizzed past him as we crossed the finish. I lost, but everyone, including me, was over the moon with my performance. A few days rest would surely be my reward.

To my utter astonishment Damien thought otherwise, his reasoning being that I was in such fine form, I was certain to go very close to winning a lower grade race in spite of the fact that I would be carrying a lot more weight, 8st 9lb to be precise. This was a claiming race remember, it meant that I would be up for grabs and I really did not want to be parted from my wonderful, loving owners, Ross and Karen. Although Damien had purchased me out of a claimer for Ross and Karen, they did not understand how the system worked and they were completely oblivious to the fact that they could now lose me in the same way, whether I won the race or came nowhere.

I really longed to be able to win a race for my great owners, I was in tip top form, why wouldn't I give it my best shot, after all, I could be claimed if I lost. My price - £4000. Besides, as I learnt previously, this would be a true test of whether their love was unerring and if they wanted to keep me.

In all honesty I was a cut above the rest of the field in this race, Chris held me up in midfield again, but this time drove me on from the 2-furlong pole and I left the others in my wake winning with ease by nearly 3 lengths. Would you believe it, I was the 11/4 favourite.

The trophy presented, now the trouble began and continued on for well over a year. Although I was at centre of it all and endured many of my own problems during that time, Ross and Karen certainly were put through the ringer.

Events unfolded in the weighing room at Southwell racecourse, where the ballot for claiming race took place, which would impinge on so many people, including myself. Ross had travelled up to Southwell on his own because work commitments precluded Karen's attendance. It was only when he arrived at the track at 11.30am, my race starting at 1pm, and was chatting with more knowledgeable racegoers in owner's bar, that Ross realised what being in a claiming race actually meant. He could lose me in the blink of an eye!

Confused and not really knowing how to proceed he rushed to the weighing room to work out what was happening. Damien, the trainer, was not able to attend that day and his assistant, David Gray had travelled down with me in the horsebox.

In the weighing room Ross discovered that my former trainer, Mark Polglase, had submitted a claim to repossess me. Clearly the General had worked out his manoeuvres with pinpoint accuracy and my former owners plan to get me back was well on track. Certainly, Ross needed to counter this offensive by putting in a "friendly claim" but, as a former Maths teacher, an even chance of keeping me was not a good option. So, with very little time to think, he concluded that the more friendly claims he put in, the better the odds of keeping me. The problem being that only one friendly claim was allowed. Without hesitation Ross filled in four more claim forms, one with Karen's name, one with David Gray's name and two other names connected to the yard. Regulations stated that all claimants needed to be present at the track and that in the event of a hostile claim succeeding the horse, i.e., me, would have to change yards for a minimum 6-month period. In theory all the claims, except that of Ross, were hostile but, of course, Ross had engineered four friendly hostile claims. That made it crystal clear to me how loved I was. For sure a lot of regulations were being broken but now Ross had a five to one (1/5, "odds on" in betting terms) chance of keeping me.

The ballot was drawn and the name David Gray came out of the hat. He was my new owner, in name only though, and Ross' strategy had paid off. There was the problem, however, of the necessity to change yards and some quick shenanigans were required to sort this out. Trainer Eric Wheeler, a friend of Damien's, was at Southwell and had the transport available to take me away, thus making the claim seem genuine. Eric agreed to take me on in his yard, running in the name of David Gray but with Ross still paying the bills. I would be moving to new accommodation in Reading, but I would still enjoy the visits and love of Ross and Karen unabated. I didn't like all the upheaval, but I knew that if it meant staying with the lovely couple who would always visit me whatever my situation. So, I was prepared to put up with the hardship.

Ross getting another photo opportunity with me

I'm in charge – as usual

CHAPTER 4

READING – NOT A FESTIVAL

Unfortunately, as it turned out, I wasn't too enamoured with my accommodation in Reading, and I never really felt at home there. I felt more of an interloper. Although I always had Ross and Karen's weekend visits to look forward to, I could never really get that settled feeling. All my friends were still at Damien's yard and I was lonely. Once again, bearing in mind that I had joined Eric's yard in top form, a repeat of what had happened to me in my younger days, resulted in a big drop in my performance levels. I believe that this was due entirely to my state of mind, to be blunt, my unhappiness.

Despite trying really hard in my first race in my new colours, coming 5th, over the next month my melancholy revealed itself in two appalling performances. Back at the yard, I knew that I was becoming quite headstrong because nothing seemed to be done to rectify my displeasure. The frustration this caused meant that I just couldn't seem to prevent bad things from happening. It was a vicious circle! I knew I had to do something, but what?

Then, one morning, completely out of the blue and without thinking, as the stable lad opened the door of my box to take me to the gallops, I slipped the rein and escaped. I bolted from my box, followed, at speed, by a panic-stricken stable lad waving his arms and shouting at me to stop. Somehow, instinctively, I also managed to find the exit from the yard before galloping down the main road, a dangerous journey which ended up with me on my backside in the middle of Reading High Street. This was an extremely scary experience even for a fearless adventurer like me. If truth be told, I was absolutely terrified and extremely lucky that I survived in one piece. But at least I had acted to end my misery and, although the whole escapade nearly ended in a total disaster, inexplicably I felt much better about myself.

As I recall, this is the actual chain of events. When I galloped down Reading High Street in blind panic, my very slippery shoes allowed me no traction and caused me to fall heavily on the tarmacked road, only yards in front of an oncoming bus which I had spotted only at the very last moment. Something that big, how could I miss it? I hadn't come into close contact with a bus before, although I had noticed them on the road as I travelled around the country, and it was a pretty daunting experience. I don't remember my heart ever beating that fast before and the images that flashed into my brain were far from pleasant. Of course, I went down on my backside with an almighty crunch, the impact resulting in a huge, and I mean huge, swelling all around my back end. Not very pretty and very painful. This swelling literally took years to be sorted out and, quite apart from the constant nagging pain during all that those years, the damage it did to my appearance was very upsetting.

Emergency services were called, and I was helped back up onto my feet by some very kind and attentive bystanders, just a few yards in front of the bus that had so brilliantly taken evasive action to avoid me. The yard had to send transport to return me to base where I spent many weeks on the naughty step. Without any doubt, I was completely ostracised by the whole population of the yard, human and animal.

Now I had another 6-months of box rest to endure in these very lonely surroundings and it was very difficult not to feel unloved. There is no doubt that, during this miserable period, my mental health came under severe strain. Also, in spite of all that convalescence time, the vets could never get to the bottom of the problem injury caused by my acrobatics, and this now manifested itself in a dinner plate size swelling over my rump. The decision was made for me to pick up my racing career again as the injury did not seem to interfere with my movement. At least getting out of that claustrophobic stable was a necessary bonus.

Just as I restarted my serious race training again, I heard that Ross was being investigated over the claims procedure that had resulted in me arriving at Reading in the first place. The racing authorities had received a complaint that he had put in more than one claim and he and Karen had been summoned to Racing HQ to face the music, a bit rough on Karen as she hadn't even been at the track that day. As this had all happened many months previously, I was gobsmacked that I yet may be dragged back to my previous owners. Fortunately, I was to find out that, although Ross was found guilty of wrongdoing and fined as the ringleader, amusing really when he was the only one in the ring, because I had served my 6 months in a new yard the ownership papers could not be altered. I remained Ross' horse – just not officially. A mass of trouble but, as I look back now, the end more than fully justified the means.

As the calendar ticked over to 2004 and my fitness for racing returned, I had a couple of lack lustre returns to the track where my 100/1 starting prices summed up my chances. Ross and Karen were always there for me, though, for better or for worse, success or failure. Probably justifiably, trainer Eric Wheeler had clearly lost patience with me and, although he was being paid my stable fees, in all likelihood he was not all that happy with Ross and Karen questioning my well-being during their weekly visits. Sure enough, I was a bit of an invalid, but these two people loved me unconditionally and I knew that.

Then, completely out of left field, and to the fury of my wonderful owners, the trainer entered me in another claiming race, ostensibly to give me a chance to improve my form in a low-grade race but, more likely, in the hope that I would be moved on.

Although Ross, in practice, could now return me to his ownership and place me in whatever yard he wanted, because of the recent proceedings at HQ it was not considered wise to do so quite so quickly.

CHAPTER 5

DONE YOU AGAIN

It was almost a year to the day since that last claiming race had caused so much kafuffle. What would today have in store? It was 29th January 2004.

Bearing in mind that my form was awful and this almighty swelling on my rear-end was severely disfiguring my beautiful body, so who in their right mind would want me, when we arrived at the track and Ross went to the weighing room to find out if anything was happening on the claiming front, he discovered that my old trainer Mark Polglase was back on the scene and had put in a claim to get me. Of course, I was still racing in David Gray's name so Ross would now have to put in a hostile claim of his own in order to get me back and save me from Mr Polglase who was clearly there out of spite. To ensure that there was no possibility of retribution Ross had definitely to put in one, and only one, claim.

The result didn't matter that day and the fact that I was rubbish, coming 5th at 50/1, was irrelevant and made it even more incredulous that anybody would want to claim me. All the horses in that race were up for grabs but I was the only one that was wanted – wanted by Ross and wanted by Mark Polglase.

It must be said that it was with some trepidation that I watched from the unsaddling enclosure as Ross and Mark walked into the weighing room to complete the draw to resolve the claim. When Ross came out of there with a beaming smile, I knew that he and Karen would be keeping me and that, as soon as possible, I would be returning to much happier surroundings at Damien's yard. That, in essence, gave Ross a three-nil tally over Mark Polglase in claiming ballots and I did smile to myself when I heard Ross' uncharacteristic remark to Mark "I've done you again!" Palpable relief oozing from every sinew of his body.

Another losing ticket: that's why they've still got it!

Bookmaker's race card

.oOo.

Although it took a couple of months because of some administrative difficulties, I absolutely loved being back at Damien Black's stable. All my old mates were still there, and it was fantastic to feel so warm and comfortable again. However, because the swelling on my back end was still giving me gyp and it was abundantly clear that I wasn't enjoying my racing, I sort of stumbled into another 5 months off. To be sure, I was in no way anywhere near earning my keep, but it didn't seem to matter a jot to Ross and Karen. I cannot in all honesty say that I didn't enjoy this latest period of rest and recuperation, repairing my severely damaged mental health being the incredible reward that this period of relaxation and mingling with old friends offered me. During those last couple of months of 2004, I had half a dozen tasters to get me back into the swing of racing and, at least, I had a good 2nd at Southwell.

However, the consequence of such a long series of poor performances was that my handicap mark dropped like a stone. If I tell you that it is very rare that a horse rated less than 45 can get into a race and that my mark fell into the 30s, indeed as low as 30 itself a couple of times, it is a wonder that I got into any races at all. Yet, would you believe it, in 2005 I set the world record for the number of times that a racehorse ran in one calendar year. 30 times! Now that is a wow! It was a fact that I seemed to get into every race that I was entered for. Grandad Nijinsky not only would have been amazed but also, I think, very proud.

I think that Ross and Karen just liked travelling round the country to watch me race, it certainly wasn't to collect trophies. I definitely didn't mind all those adventures. It meant that I did all my training on the racecourse itself and bypassed all that boring work on the gallops. The reason I got to run so many times in that year was quite astounding really. Because I was so bad, I was entered in every race possible to ensure that I got into an odd race every now and again. The staggering coincidences of wrong going, bad weather and lack of entries conspired to ensure that, quite unbelievably, I got into almost every race I was entered for.

My itinerary was most impressive. Besides running 19 of my 30 races at my beloved Southwell, I did get to run at the Mecca of racing, Goodwood, where I came a creditable 13th (of course) of 20 at 33/1. During this halcyon period, I actually won a race at Southwell, ridden by 7lb claimer Laura Reynolds – as you know I loved being ridden by apprentice jockeys.

I stayed nice and busy during early 2006 and my handicap was on the rise again, enabling me to get an upgrade from class 7 races to the nose bleedingly heights of class 6 handicaps. Just like being back in the times when I was, or could have been, very good.

Another win. Ross and Karen with my apprentice jockey Laura

CHAPTER 6

ON THE RADIO

On 16th February 2006 I arrived at Southwell for my latest spin around that fibresand paradise. As I checked into my designated holding box, I got wind of some serious chatter around the stable block concerning the rumour that BBC Radio 4 being present. They were going to do a piece on their flagship 5 o'clock news programme about all-weather racing, its popularity and why owners seemed to love it so much. This was an opportunity for me to hit the big time. I needed to get my proper race head on.

Here I was at Southwell. Right time, right place. My favourite track, my favourite distance - one mile - an apprentice race with me allotted the least experienced jockey in the field - Tolley Dean - a young lad riding someone as good as me for the first time. Time for me to show him the ropes and kick start his career. Add to all this that my great mate from Damien's yard, Supreme Salutation, another lucky horse because he too was owned by Ross and Karen, not only had travelled up with me in the horsebox but also was in the very same race as me. Talk about being relaxed about the situation, I was almost horizontal. I couldn't have been any happier. Even on top of all that, I was 22/1 so nobody expected me to put in any kind of performance — except Ross that is who, I knew full well, would stick £100 on me to win. Supreme Salutation was only 10/1 in this race, but we both knew that I had the better chance.

It turned out to be exactly my type of race. I let Tolley believe that he was tracking the leading group of horses but, be in no doubt, it was me who was doing the steering. With a furlong to go I thought – *this is it, radio stardom here I come*. I stepped out to the centre of the track and really let rip, pulling away by a length or more and winning with loads of energy to spare. I could be brilliant when the mood took me, and I was fantastic that day. I could hear Ross' bellowing voice shouting me home all the way round the track and this told me that not only was he well pleased but also, he would attract the attention of the radio reporter.

So as we went into the winner's enclosure to receive our trophy, I knew that I was to become a radio superstar. Ross was, indeed, extricated from the celebrations to do a fifteen-minute interview on Radio 4 primetime in which he gave a wonderful eulogy of my quite superb performance. I was so very pleased, not only for myself, but also for Ross whose devotion to me, along with that of Karen, definitely merited such a joyful reward. The £2200 winnings collected from a very upset bookmaker helped a bit as well.

On the trip back home along with Supreme Salutation in the horse box, I reflected on how brilliant I might have been with consistent effort. Unfortunately, life intervenes and your mood, happy or sad, unquestionably affects how you perform. My career statistics ended up with me running in 117 races of which I won 8 and was placed on 18 other occasions. In money I won £26,745, though it's probably best not to say how much it cost to keep me over the years.

Soon after that success however, I sustained another nasty knock which caused me to retire, permanently I thought, from racing. Ross and Karen's great friend Mike Murphy had set up a training stables of his own in Westoning and, because I was everybody's favourite, he agreed to let me holiday at his place and enjoy life a little bit. Actually, I was off for 347 days and, do you know, not a single vet could fathom out how to treat the still bothersome swelling on my rear. How many years was that?

In early 2007, I seemed really happy with myself and was getting a trifle bored. As I was still only 9 years old the consensus was that perhaps I should give racing another go. Another change of scenery saw Ross and Karen lodging me with their new trainer, Nick Littmoden, at Newmarket. I would be living on Hamilton Road, in a beautiful racing yard adjacent to the marvellous Newmarket gallops.

Winner's enclosure once again. Denise, Ross and Karen with me and the stable lad, Mike and Milly

A few weeks of training in such an idyllic setting saw me regain all my enthusiasm for the game and in my comeback run at Southwell on 8th February 2007 I came 2nd of 10 at the miserly starting price of 11/1, considering I'd been off the track for a year. Immediately my handicap mark soared into the 50s. Then, to my absolute joy, my young friend from Damien's yard, the ridiculously talented Lord Theo, arrived at Nick's yard to further his career. To be reunited with such a great mate was a fantastic bonus and I really was very, very happy.

I made the frame on a couple more occasions before, in May 2007, at an evening race at Kempton Park, it became apparent not only to me but also to all my connections that perhaps my heart wasn't totally into racing anymore. As said, this was an evening meeting, which was entirely a new experience for me. Another surprise to me was the massive TV screen set up at the furlong pole in the home straight. I'd never seen anything like that before and it was oh so bright in the evening gloom. That night, I had champion jockey Seb Sanders riding me so, obviously he thought that he was in charge when he brought me to challenge for the lead at the 3-furlong pole. Do you know what, all I could think about was that screen and, looking up, what struck me was this magnificent chestnut with a beautiful white face steaming down the home straight. It was me! What a fantastic looking animal, I thought, totally forgetting that I was running in a thing called a race and just immersing myself in a moment of ultimate pleasure and self-admiration.

Of course, I trailed in almost last and the afore mentioned jockey was not in the slightest bit amused, throwing his saddle, with some venom, onto the floor almost before he had completed his dismount in a display of complete exasperation,

This moment sort of began to sum up my state of mind and, after a leisurely stroll round Yarmouth Racecourse a few weeks later, all of my fans agreed that it was time to lower the curtain on my racing exploits. I had had a blast. Everybody loved me, I had set a world record and become a star of radio and screen.

It was time for Ross and Karen to find me a retirement home. Where would that be and what would it be like?

Farewell racing

25

CHAPTER 7

THE RIGHT CONNECTIONS

During the first nine plus years of my life, I certainly had enjoyed my fair share of ups and downs, successes and failures, plus a great deal of mischievous fun. I was always lucky enough to have been well looked after, this guaranteed after my baby years by my terrific and loving owners, Ross and Karen. At my final racing yard, for sure I had struck it lucky yet again because, not only was I based in the blissful surroundings of the hallowed turf at Newmarket, but also my last trainer, Nick Littmoden, was not only a wonderfully caring horseman but also knew how important it was for caring owners to know that old has-beens like me would have a well-cared for and happy life in retirement.

Lucky Kumakawa had struck gold yet again because there were two wonderful girls working at Nick's yard who, it turned out, would know just the angel to look after me. Suzanne Dickens and Cheryl Marshall were the fabulous ladies in my life at the right time, in the right place and with the best connections ever. Suzanne, particularly, had a lot of experience on the racehorse circuit and knew a lot of fantastic people. She and Cheryl put their heads together and they came up with the perfect answer for my future happiness.

They absolutely knew that someone as very strong minded and quirky as myself would require a very patient, yet firm, knowledgeable, and equally strong-minded carer to take charge of my retirement. So it was that they got in touch with an old friend from their previous days on the road - a lovely lady from the Newport area of South Wales, to see if she might be interested in taking me on. Her name – Helen McCarthy.

To say that it was love at first sight is the understatement of all time! She completely fell for me, hook, line and sinker! To be fair – I felt exactly the same.

If ever there could be one, this was a match made in heaven and I knew, to the very bottom of my heart, that my very own Guardian Angel had been sent from above to protect and guide me for the rest of my life. I believe wholeheartedly that Helen was created, especially to look after me and, although I can't help being naughty sometimes, I value every second that I spend with her, and I only hope that I bring her a modicum of joy to go along with all the concerns that I give to her.

I shall forever be in the debt of Suzanne and Cheryl for finding me such an amazing home with such a special angel.

Now my life was in for a major culture change and my latest long distance horsebox ride would be all the way to Newport and the beautiful landscape of South Wales. Let's see what Helen has in store for me.

.oOo.

It was a most beautiful summer's day, on Sunday 12th August 2007. On my second meeting with Helen, she arrived at Nick's yard in Newmarket driving a horsebox, luxuriously fitted with all the amenities to ensure that my long journey to Wales would be extremely comfortable. I particularly remember that the hay on board was of exceedingly good quality – funny how those little things stick in your mind, especially during life changing moments. We were heading for Bassaleg in South Wales. Bassaleg is a suburb on the west side of Newport, only some 2 miles from the city centre yet very countrified in the area where I would be living.

Suzanne and Cheryl were on hand to wave me a tearful goodbye while Ross and Karen couldn't handle the emotion of our parting and decided to give this departure on my last journey as a racehorse a miss.

My own sentiments were all over the place, excited to be on the road to a new life yet concerned at what prospects lay ahead. Nervous and ecstatic simultaneously. Inevitably, the journey seemed to flash by in a split second in time and, before I could in any way fully comprehend what was happening, we had arrived at our destination. As Helen helped me out of the horsebox, my overriding and most lasting impression of my new home was how peaceful it was. Just a few stables in a sea of green grass. None of the hustle and bustle of a working racing yard – eons away from everything that I had become accustomed to during my whole life. A beautiful rural setting of peace and tranquillity, all presided over by an angel – it really couldn't get much better.

However, I am Kumakawa and sometimes I failed to realise that utopia has to be earned as well as being enjoyed. This wonderful new experience mirrored a child being unleashed uncontrollably in a sweetshop. After a few days settling into my new stable, to my absolute joy, I realised that the majority of my time would be spent enjoying the freedom of the hills with a fairly large group of other horses who were stabled at various yards around the area. Looking back now, it is not surprising that I found all this a little bit too exciting for my own good. Clearly my whole background had never allowed me to learn about being the herd animal that my genes said that I was and becoming a member of such a group on those fantastic hillsides became a real challenge for me. The upshot of this tremendous fresh lifestyle basically meant that I had too much play time in the fields with my new mates, the result being, of course, that I consistently kept losing my shoes. This certainly did not endear me to my lovely Helen. Horseshoes and the job of attaching them to my feet was not a cheap option.

Sunday 12th August 2007, I arrive in Wales

Helen told me later that her farrier, Sam Rooney, son of Tim who had shod Helen's ponies when she was a young girl, became known as the 5th emergency service (police, ambulance, fire, vet and farrier). How embarrassing was that. Good job I didn't realise that at the time, I would have been mortified. I must admit, I was a bit of a drama queen at that time, behaviour which I believed would make sure that Sam came as quickly as possible to put my shoes back on.

I heard him say to Helen once that I behaved as though I had broken my leg when I had lost a shoe. That's a bit unfair, it really hurt.

I must admit that I was so lucky that Sam was very patient with me, considering that he hardly knew me, especially when I found it great fun to chew his leather chaps, hair and bandana. Hey, I'm Kumakawa, I can take my coat off and my super teeth can chew anything I want them to, clothing, wooden fences, flesh etc. I suppose Sam sort of got his own back by always referring to me as "The Princess and the Pea" because of my low pain threshold. Purely his view, you understand.

By October 2007, I was finally getting to know what Helen expected of me and her routine had made quite a few adjustments to my behaviour. I was beginning to feel really laid back, finally able to enjoy the idyllic surroundings that were my dream come true.

Unfortunately, I fell ill and became really under the weather. I had been hit with a bout of colic, so often fatal to horses. I knew things were pretty bad because Helen was absolutely hysterical with fear and panic. Again, how amazingly lucky was I to be in the care of such an incredible human being. Helen, without a second thought, immediately got me a referral to Langford (Bristol University Vet Hospital) on this, a Saturday evening. With help she got me onto the trailer for the trip to Bristol and, do you know what, whether it was the bouncing up and down of the trailer on the road or the stop starting in the traffic, but by the time we arrived at Bristol, I walked off the trailer as fit as a flea. Apparently, there is an old adage that a trailer ride can often resolve a painful colic, thank goodness, it did so in this case.

I was kept in the hospital overnight for observation and, according to the nurses, I did make a bit of a nuisance of myself but at least it did mean that I was sent home pretty quickly after all the checks confirmed that I was OK. I must say, I did lose a lot of weight following this incident and it took me quite a while to regain my good looks.

CHAPTER 8

THE EX-RACERS CLUB

By 2008 things had begun to go really well again, I was happy, enjoyed playing sensibly with my mates and was really immersing myself in a lovely lazy life. Helen brightened my days by taking me out for scenic rides exploring the hills and dales and she coupled this with teaching me lots of new skills, would you believe walking, trotting and cantering, with me expected to do these to order. Remember, I am Kumakawa, I don't take kindly to obeying instructions. I tried very hard to please Helen although, I must say, I was a little bit miffed when, out of the blue, she told me that we had become members of the Ex-Racers Club. This had the feeling of taking me back to my previous life, a total misconception on my part. Anyway, we were going to make our debut at a parade in memory of an ex-member, Sian O'Gorman. This was being held at the prestigious Newbury Racecourse, and yes, I had been there before in my previous life.

Not many people realise that horses have incredible memories and being an incredible horse, I have an extra-special incredible memory, especially when it comes to bad experiences. Newbury Racecourse had inflicted on me one of those unpleasant events.

Way back in 2001, on the 19th December to be precise, when I was still in the care of my second trainer, Mark Polglase, Newbury was the location of one of those 2-mile hurdle races which he dispatched me to. This was a race in which I struggled to complete the course, coming 13th (of course) and beaten by 190 lengths – now that is a very long way! *Enjoyment* it was not, *misery* being a far more descriptive word. This was a memory etched on my brain.

As soon as Helen got me off the trailer I knew where we were, and the bad vibes zig zagged through my whole body. I certainly was not in the right frame of mind for a parade. But parade we did. I knew I was being a nightmare for poor Helen, but my mind wasn't straight and I just couldn't concentrate on walking properly. My walking, jogging and trotting sort of all got mixed up together and we ended up going sideways around the parade ring. I certainly wasn't doing much for the decorum of the event and I heard someone say that I was the naughtiest ex-racer that they had ever seen. I was well aware that I had upset Helen and probably put her off trying anything nice with me again, but she obviously didn't know anything about my bad memories concerning Newbury. We returned to Bassaleg with our tails firmly between our legs.

Luckily for me, by the middle of summer 2008, Helen had got her mojo back and had, for some unaccountable reason, formed some kind of plan for my activities going forward. I knew she was into her internet and was in touch with Ex-Racehorse Club owners all over the country – I had no clue as to what a big organisation this was. Helen discovered that The ERC (Ex-Racehorse Club) held a championship show each year, entry to which demanded a regional qualification for your area. For some unaccountable and inexplicable reason Helen decided to take me to Chard Show in Taunton for my first show classes. "Show Classes?" – I only just learned to walk for goodness' sake, the other bits and pieces I'd practised were just that, bits and pieces. The two classes I were entered in were both qualifiers for the championship – Helen sure was expecting a lot of me.

Could I deliver? Legendary status awaited!

The first competition was being led in hand, the second a beginners ridden class – beginner defined as a former racehorse having retired from racing less than 3 years prior.

Well, when I arrived at the show ring my eyes nearly popped out of my head on stalks. There were horses and children's' ponies doing things that I had never seen before. I struggled to get my head around it all. How would I fit into this circus? I could feel Helen's excited anticipation as she met up with internet friends, some of whom had entries in the same events as me, and it was wonderfully noticeable how much support and encouragement they all offered to each other.

As per usual, the excitement was boiling up in me too and I wasn't the easiest of animals to control. I was heading for the "in hand class" in a very bouncy frame of mind at the same time as the previous class was just finishing, the horses having been awarded their rosettes and embarking on their lap of honour with spectators clapping.

Now this was really exciting. Laps of honour – just up my street. I reared up and escaped Helen's clutches and was free to show exactly what I could do. Wreaking havoc was the unseemly outcome. Shades of Reading flooded back into my mind as I raced in the opposite direction of the show ground, luckily for everybody else, horses and competitors alike, this time avoiding a busy main road but, nevertheless, ending up in a very muddy farmer's field which, conveniently, afforded me the chance of an extremely fast gallop to its farthest corner, where I paused for thought.

I did look very smart in all my fine show apparel and, I must say, so did Helen, in all her finest equine gear, as she traipsed across the mud to collect me, although her demeanour didn't appear to display many fine thoughts. I had certainly earned that legendary status. New kid on the block and everyone knew exactly who I was.

Believe it or not, when Helen got me back to the show ring for that "in hand" class, I came 2nd. Whether it was the shock of my experience, or the exhaustion caused by it, I behaved with impeccable sobriety and made myself (and hopefully Helen) proud. Not for long though, I wasn't very good at all in "the ridden" class which, I know was a big disappointment to Helen. She probably thought she had made a mistake taking me that far to a big show ring when I was a bit inexperienced, but we all live and learn. Hey, I achieved legendary status (as always) and Helen got some brilliant photographs.

.oOo.

As 2009 clicked into place, I soon realised that Helen undoubtedly meant business. I knew by now that this amazing lady had reached the ultimate heights in her academic career and had a burning ambition to unleash all my hidden potential as a horse in just about every horse discipline you could think of – dressage, showing, show jumping, eventing, you name it, plus of course as much hacking as any free time would allow.

I certainly was up for giving it my all, how could anyone resist the infectious competitive spirit of Helen, but I worried that my limitations and proneness to being a bit naughty might let her down. Nevertheless, together, we really got down to business. This would be a challenge for both of us.

Helen had fantastic connections throughout the equine fraternity, she had lots of horse friends who helped us with their facilities and it was at our local riding club where I learned how to show jump, a skill that was a must in order for me to progress to cross-country. I did particularly enjoy the dressage training when I finally realised that, with masses of concentration, I could actually do as I was told for quite a long period of time.

These newly developing skills definitely helped me when I tried show jumping – a pity that I hadn't had them at my disposal during my ill-fated hurdling attempts as a racehorse. Hurdling and show jumping were worlds apart, in hurdling you are as free as a bird whereas show jumping meant having to learn to jump in a small space, in a very controlled and steady manner. Plenty of practice made sure that I got better and better and I was extremely pleased with my development into such a talented animal.

We were incredibly lucky again to have Helen's friend, Debby, join us on our show jumping and cross-country adventures. These were such fun times. Debby's horse Benji was a real sweetie and a horse that inspired confidence in both me and Helen. He was totally unafraid and would jump anything, so brave. He and Debby would give Helen and I a lead and we would have to copy him - becoming "a flying couple".

I loved Benji to bits and, out of respect, never even thought about racing him or overtaking him, knowing full well that my prowess as a speedster racehorse was never in any doubt.

Apparently, Helen was extremely pleased with my progress in re-training, and she set us the target of appearing in a couple of local showing events, victory in either of which would launch us into the stratospheric heights of competing in the Retraining of Racehorses (RoR) final at the awe-inspiring venue of Hickstead.

To be honest, I was very nervous, at the same time excited, about all this but, when we arrived at the first event, I was actually over the moon, especially as both Helen and I looked so very smart in all our equine finery.

I know that Helen was extremely worried that the whole experience might have come a bit early in my new career path and I, myself, was concerned that my excitement could transcend into uncontrollable exuberance.

I worried that, as Helen revelled in the excitement and pleasure of events like these, sadly, it wouldn't be long before the very naughty Kumakawa surfaced and put a damper on the whole event. Today's show involved walking, trotting and cantering around the arena at the same time as other racehorses. Just to put a bit of spice into the mix, on this occasion the judge would actually ride each horse for a few circuits of the arena. I'm afraid that this hadn't been factored into my thinking.

For me, judge = top jockey, top jockeys think they know it all and decide how the ride will go. I've always been crystal clear that, throughout my racing career, this does not apply to me. Imagine the embarrassment for all concerned when the judge, after barely one lap, decided, for her own safety, to dismount and retreat to her podium. I still can't quite believe that she placed me last that day, I was pretty good at everything else.

To be fair, I am almost certain that stress, combined with the excitement of everything that was happening, played a big role in my temperamental misdemeanours. I wasn't 100% sure of what was actually expected of me and I allowed the special atmosphere of these large events to get to me although, sometimes, the arrangements at the shows themselves didn't help the situation.

Interspersed with all this training and the competitions that it all leads to, were the many injuries and illnesses which I picked up while enjoying myself in the picturesque surroundings of South Wales. Not only must this have been very frustrating for Helen but also caused her non-stop expense. As the recipient of all this medical care and time-consuming tenderness, little did I realise the stress and strain that this was imposing on my most wonderful owner. At least when I was racing, I won the odd bit of prize money to help with the finances, but I felt guilty that I was spending an inordinate amount of time with the vet.

As well as lots of little scrapes, I got a nasty injury to my left cheek that caused a lot of concern, and this was followed by a bout of mud fever. This is a bacterial infection normally associated with the winter but of course I, the inimitable Kumakawa, got it in the summer. I am so, so special. Poor Helen had to give me a daily leg wash which, combined with prescribed medication, went on for weeks on end. All this in the stable – no chance of getting in the field, having to stay socially distanced from my mates.

Of course, when I returned to full health, ready for some serious exercise after weeks caged up, I was literally "champing at the bit" and "fresh" was a very understated adjective to describe my state of mind. Helen was desperate to undertake the enormous challenge of riding out this powerful, equine machine and I loved the feeling of having her on my back once again. She was an angel, my shining star and I would do anything for her. Yet, to my utter horror and dismay, I proved too strong and unstable for her after all that time off and this resulted in her taking a nasty fall, causing one of her arms to become a bit of a mess. I was utterly crestfallen and bearing responsibility for this accident weighed heavily on my mind. I feel that responsibility even today when, in good weather, I can still see the scars of that incident etched on Helen's arm, from her hand right up to her elbow. It's so true that you always hurt the one you love.

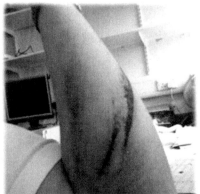

OUCH!

CHAPTER 9

MORE TROUBLE - BUT WITH A SILVER LINING

Now we were off on another expedition, this time to the Chepstow Agricultural Show. This was a bit different in that it was billed as an educational experience for ex racehorses. Unfortunately, although with the very best of intentions, the hosts had decided to hold these classes in the main show ring – a quite acceptable decision one would have thought, bearing in mind the experience element of the exercise.

Clearly, the hosts desire to make a big thing of this display carried little or no influence with me and I could feel Helen's nervousness, nay fear, about how I would behave. For some unaccountable reason I have this streak of total mayhem sewn into my psyche and, no matter how hard I try, I cannot stop it getting out. I really don't mean to be a pain, but I know that I am.

Every fibre of my being knew that Helen was fearing the worst, neither of us knew quite how bad things would be. Think of a superlative for the word bad and you'll get somewhere near it.

What planet are the organisers of such events on when, in order to get to the main ring, first I was taken through the car park in order to get to the next field. I kid you not, next I had to breeze past the Helter Skelter, The Bouncy Castle and a whole host of other children's attractions. I was here to experience show classes, for goodness' sake, not to have a go on the fair. Not only did I find these features themselves to be a massive issue, but poor Helen had to struggle negotiating mums with pushchairs and prams while I was getting higher than a helium balloon. I had to close my ears in order to avoid hearing Helen utter words I really didn't think she knew, as finally, we proceeded to enter into our own Colosseum. Not much education today, I thought.

You could not make it up but, as we circled the show ring to complete each separate class, on each circuit we had to pass by the Member's Marquee, nice view for them but, for us, inconveniently situated alongside the ring. Seriously, had anyone considered my presence? I'm not sure if it was an unlucky coincidence or just pure devilment but, each time we went past that marquee and its illustrious viewing guests, it appeared that every possible waiter or kitchen assistant was either scraping plates clean or banging saucepans together in a crescendo of noise that would have put an NHS clap to shame. Not an experience to be repeated as I now demonstrated, without question, clearly exemplifying how not to behave in a show ring. Poor Helen and Kumakawa were becoming both notorious and legendary very quickly indeed.

Putting these experiences firmly behind us and with a desire to move forward with our characteristic optimism, in December 2009 Helen made the decision for us to change yards. For some reason I seemed to be picking up a lot of niggling injuries in our current home and the grazing and general facilities were not all that brilliant. So it was that we packed our bags and moved a few miles up the road to a small hamlet near Risca. This was a small private yard with just 5 other horses owned by a lovely lady named Nicola. I knew that Helen thought that this yard would provide me with a much safer environment and minimise my injuries, injuries that always put such a strain on her purse strings.

Having said that, it was now that my silver lining arrived and, coincidentally, all because of an injury I sustained almost immediately I arrived at my new home. On arrival I was introduced to my two new field mates, Fly, a mare, and Scruffy, a gelding. Obviously, with one girl and two boys in a field, there was bound to be an initial tussle for the alpha male spot, and I wasn't quite the champion I thought I was. Scruffy was a tough street fighter and he wanted to preserve his special relationship with Fly, making sure that I knew exactly where my position was in the horse hierarchy.

To let me know absolutely where I stood, Scruffy landed an extremely hard kick on my back end, leaving me in no doubt as to his feelings. This kick landed squarely on the lump that I had sustained in my incident on Reading High Street all that time ago. This unsightly blemish on my otherwise beautiful body had remained incurable for years. No vet, no treatment, no anything had ever managed to solve its mystery. To cut a long story short, this vehement kick must have dislodged something inside the lump which caused it, almost immediately, to grow in size before bursting like bomb on New Year's Day, 2010, not the cheapest time for yet another vet call-out.

Scruffy, Fly and me Christmas 2009

Always putting me first, Helen did not hesitate to get the necessary emergency treatment under way and none of us, me, the vet or Helen, could believe the massive build-up of puss that had been festering for so long. What a martyr I must have been to exist with all that poison in my body for such a long time. Hero, or what? Now Helen had to make sure to flush out the wound every day with saline while I endured a complete course of antibiotics. I can squeamishly remember Helen pressing and squeezing the bump as she used the saline wash, seeing the odious smelling puss squirt out to a distance of 8 inches or more. Such a good job that she had such a strong constitution.

That was my fantastic silver lining. Many thanks to Scruffy for seeing to it that I entered 2010 with a body back to being fit for the super handsome animal that I am. Amazing gratitude to Helen, also, for being there for me yet again in spite of all the problems that I didn't really mean to cause her.

CHAPTER 10

THE DRESSAGE CONUNDRUM

We were really enjoying life at our new home. Blue House Farm, where we were based, was a lovely place in which to de-stress and somewhere where we could immerse ourselves completely in the relaxing country life. I had built up a brilliant relationship with Helen's lovely border collie dog, Leah. She was a steadfast friend and there was just something so special between us. We did everything together and she would be by my side at every possible opportunity, running many miles with me giving me her invaluable and much appreciated support.

With all these amazingly positive factors in my favour, you would have thought that I would be in the right frame of mind to have a real go at making some progress in becoming either a dressage horse or a jumper, or both. I thoroughly enjoyed all the hard work but probably I enjoyed it all a little bit too much. My exuberance was a definite negative in the scheme of things and it must have been a real disappointment to Helen that, in spite of all the promise I was undoubtedly showing, I would probably fall between the two stools and not be good enough at either discipline.

First of all, let's examine the dressage side of things.

It was quite clear to me that Helen really wanted me to be a top dressage horse. I most definitely had the good looks and poise to make an instant impression with any judge and I certainly had the brain power to carry out any allotted task. The problem for me was that to be a dressage horse you need to demonstrate submission and, of course, this is something I have struggled with for the whole of my life.

I have always desired to do things my own way. This is something that I can, with certainty, relate way back to my early racing days when race jockeys seemed to have not an inkling as to what I was all about and, most seriously of all, not have the faintest clue as to what was best for me and, therefore, how to get the best out of me. From those youthful days I developed a strong sense of self preservation and a personality that very much put the onus on self-determination and self-decision making.

I did good!

Smiler!

With regard to dressage, if you watch the great Valegro and Charlotte Dujardin, they work in perfect harmony with not a single disagreement evident. For some unaccountable reason, I always seemed to struggle to cooperate with Helen. I knew I was making life difficult for her, especially when I got into the terrible habit of tossing my head around to the extreme. I really can't explain why I behaved in this way and, when Leah (my first collie dog companion) questioned me as to what was going on, neither of us could decide whether it was disobedience, stress or plain stubbornness. All of these terrible faults were unquestionably in my armoury – none with any malice aforethought I must most clearly assert.

Helen, however, refused to give up on the dressage dream and she spent an inordinate amount of time, effort and money on the project. She received great help and advice from top trainers such as Sally Williams and Jacky Leonard but they too experienced deep frustration when I let them down after initially showing fantastic promise. Poor Helen took it on herself to make me appear a lot better than I actually was, whether through misplaced pride or embarrassment I really don't know. She would show to her friends incredible still frames of my dressage performances, having carefully edited them from videos of the events. These were super impressive but, in reality, all taken from pretty abysmal displays. I felt so badly for Helen, always doing her utmost to make me look so much better than I was.

I often overheard her friends telling her that she did too much for me – they were absolutely right, of course. Headstrong and naughty, for whatever reason I always had to do it my way. I do believe that that Frank Sinatra song was written especially about me.

Despite all these disappointments and false dawns, Helen persisted in taking me dressage training and also to some competitions. I suppose she was as stubborn as me. We visited The David Broome Event Centre in Chepstow many times over the years, and it is fair to say that I definitely left my mark on the memories of many competitors, horses and judges alike. As usual all the photographic evidence is fabulous but, in reality, the horrendous legends are nearly always true. Suffice it to say, fame has most certainly touched me.

.oOo.

Given that I was challenging Helen rather a bit too much in the dressage department, she decided to give me a real good go at jumping, both show jumping and cross country. This was right up my street, and I enjoyed every second. I built on those early training sessions I had undertaken when I first arrived in Wales, when Helen had succeeded in banishing all those demons I had left over from my sad experiences over hurdles as a racehorse.

Now I was full of confidence and felt as free as a bird as I hurtled over the fences. I absolutely loved every minute of it and really had almost too much fun. I thoroughly relished the thought that it was me putting Helen through her paces this time, using my amazing strength to almost pull her arms out of their sockets while, simultaneously, forcing on-lookers to reach for the smelling salts as I tackled my fences at top speed. My adventures with Benji had taught me to show no fear and, boy, did I revel in the bravery of it all.

Unsurprisingly there was, of course, a tiny downside to this life of adventure. Sometimes a fence would loom up that I didn't quite fancy. If they don't want to jump, most horses simply stop dead in front of the jump. I've got my own method, though, probably because I don't make up my mind about what I am going to do until the last millisecond. My system involves stopping momentarily, then violently swerving either left or right, according to convenience, which invariably causes my rider, Helen of course, to be deposited firmly and at speed upon the ground. Not good. I particularly remember this happening at a Wye Valley Training Day in July 2010. After I had dispatched Helen to her fate, I performed a stunning lap of honour around the field, to be followed by several more before being cornered and hauled in by rather a lot of disgruntled horse people.

Naturally this wasn't the only time that events proceeded to this outcome. When we were Cross country training at Sunnybank Equestrian Centre in Caerphilly, another of our frequently visited venues, some misguided official had made the insane decision to situate some most unpleasant and threatening porta-loos right on the course itself. Sadly, I wasn't prepared to endure the danger of these unsightly edifices but, as I spun to return to the safety of the stabling area, I forgot to take Helen with me. I abandoned her without thought and I am still totally embarrassed by the whole episode. At least the toilets were nearby.

Although, palpably, I deserved little or no reward for all my colourful exploits during 2010, nevertheless Helen decided to give me the joy of a visit to the beach. She did have some serious reservations about this excursion because, remember, I had spent many hours during my racing career circling the sand racetrack at Southwell Racecourse and at very high speed. I'm sure that Helen, and the friend that helped her with me that day, didn't expect me to notice the actual sea, a quite distinct difference to the landscape at Southwell.

Why everyone was surprised at my calm behaviour I'll never fathom, but as long as I didn't have to get my feet wet, all would remain absolutely serene. However, it wasn't for the want of trying that I managed to stay dry, Helen thought it would be a hoot to get me wet but I wasn't prepared to play ball. The beach we went to was Kenfig, a huge beach and one that was very quiet and peaceful on a weekday. Perfect.

It was so sensible that the pair had brought me to the beach on my own. The sand was so wonderful to run on that I know I would have got carried away and raced like lightening if I was in tandem with another horse. Being alone, I was able fully to take in the wonderful surroundings, the sun, the sea, the air.

Helen was ecstatic that seemingly I could behave like a total gentleman and we were able to canter up and down the beach with her in complete control. This is exactly how I wanted things to be. No pressure of performing, no crowds, no over mighty judges and no nasty porta-loos. I was completely relaxed and loving every second of this experience. The tide was ebbing further outwards, and the dry sand was so wonderful to run on. Ross and Karen had always told Helen that they thought I would have run well on firm ground – I think that they were right.

The other, often overlooked but oh so important, main ingredient to my complete serenity that day was the fact that my ever-faithful friend Leah, Helen's amazing and gorgeous collie, ran every step of the way behind me. As I said earlier, ours was a relationship made in heaven and we valued every single second we spent in each other's company.

This was a very special day; I shall remember it forever. Yet another unbelievable debt that I owe to my quite incredible owner.

CHAPTER 11

WOOD ADDICT – FULL DISCLOSURE

Now, as I look back on the wonderful time I have spent in Wales, it seems right that, at this juncture, I should reflect on the bad habits that have, shall we say, not covered me in glory.

As, at the age of 24, I am writing this biography in real time, 2022, I feel that I should face my demons head on as, embarrassingly, my main obsession reared its ugly head again on this actual day.

I am, and apparently always have been, a windsucker. As a result of this behaviour, I have become addicted to wood. I cannot resist wrapping my mouth around anything wooden, be it fenceposts, gates or stable doors, anything to satisfy my habit. I am trying to be frank and open in this admission and, although full of regret, I have never managed to overcome the habit despite the anguish and constant misery that it has caused to the person I love most in the world, Helen.

What is windsucking? Windsucking, or crib biting, is a stereotypical behaviour specific to horses. Its definition is a repetitive behaviour that has no function. In my case, along with most horses, windsucking manifests itself by me clamping my mouth onto anything wooden and then gulping in air. Of course, these actions have been far from beneficial to my teeth and also have given me lots of muscle pain in my neck area as I tense up to suck the air in. This has a knock-on effect to my shoulders but, even with all that unpleasant pain, I have not been able to overcome this nasty affliction. When Helen has brought in experts to advise on my addiction, I have overheard them say that repetitive windsucking has been shown to provide feel good hormones, called endorphins, to the horse and this makes it almost impossible to correct the problem.

Zoo animals often exhibit this type of behaviour due to confinement and one belief is that it develops in horses from being stabled too long. Another opinion as to its cause is that a horse will learn this behaviour from another by imitation – whatever the case, I openly admit that I suffer from it.

The big question is, did I behave in this way when I was a racehorse? Could this be a reason as to why I was unpopular in certain yards? Windsuckers are extremely unpopular in the equine world. As Helen says, "It's almost like you have the most contagious disease on the planet, no one wants you and your horse is a bad influence on others." Honestly, I am so, so sorry that my will is not strong enough to put this problem to bed. I hope that this open and frank admission that I have a bad habit will, at least, be a step in the right direction.

In all truthfulness, I cannot say for certain whether I used to windsuck as a racehorse. Of course, in all probability I did, although not at a time when Ross and Karen, my then wonderful owners, would have noticed anything strange. They tended to see me always at my best on their visits and, also, I would be working on the gallops for most of the time that they were in the yard. When I was on rest and recuperation time, Karen would always spoil me with Extra Strong Mints and carrots so there was no need for me to chase the pleasures of other endorphins.

Certainly, when Helen came to meet me at Nick Littmoden's yard at Newmarket all those years ago and she rode me out, we just had great fun and, when we returned to the stable, she was not informed that I had any problems or bad habits. I am sure that one of the girls, either Cheryl or Suzanne, would have mentioned anything that they thought might cause Helen any difficulties. It must have been such a crushing blow to Helen when, 24 hours later, after a lovely journey to South Wales and a comfortable first night in my new home, I completely messed everything up. At the same time as Helen was on her way from her home to give me my breakfast, a journey barely lasting 15 minutes, I disgraced us both by making my first act at the stable an episode of windsucking.

My new home consisted of an American barn system where lots of horses were stabled together. Obviously, the whole situation was a completely new routine for me. Back in Newmarket we were all fed at the same time, no waiting about and craving for what the others were having for breakfast. So, for whatever reason, as I saw others being fed while I had nothing to eat, I clenched my teeth onto the stable door and began to windsuck. I could say that the motivation was that all the others were having their breakfast before me but being honest, I must have exhibited this behaviour before, I simply hadn't been at this stable long enough to copy anyone. I suppose, tongue in cheek, Helen might have helped matters by getting up earlier that day – or feeding me first!

How embarrassed was I when Helen arrived at the livery to face a barrage of insults and abuse, all caused by the wild panic experienced by other horse owners and livery yard owners when a windsucker comes into their midst. Like many in the equine world, they believe that windsucking is imitative behaviour that spreads like the plague. Not proven, by the way.

Suffice it to say that the pair of us barely lasted two weeks in this hostile environment. Helen moved me up the road to Dave Harris's yard. Dave was much more tolerant of my behaviour and, thank goodness, Helen was able to ditch the cribbing collar that she was forced to fit on me at the previous gulag. Cribbing collars are horrendous things, fitting so tightly around your neck that they rub dreadfully and just aggravate the wearer rather than correct their behaviour. Research has also shown, I have heard, that forcibly denying windsucking horses of this habit can in fact be detrimental to their health and wellbeing.

But then I'm Kumakawa - there's always an excuse for me!

With the dreaded collar discarded, a new solution had to be found. It manifested itself in a product called Cribox. Helen used this mercilessly to

48

keep me away from the wooden fence rails. It is a horrendously dark, sticky and smelly substance, an affront to any horse and a source of more trouble for Helen when other horse owners got it on their clothes. The money that woman must have spent and the flak she must have taken! And still is taking, by the way.

.oOo.

When we moved to Blue House farm, which is about where we are in our true life-story, things were so much more relaxed. My favourite place to windsuck was on my feed manger inside the stable. Nic, the farm owner, and her husband Simon were wonderfully supportive, and I so appreciated everything that they did to try to help me and stop me from getting into trouble. With my predisposition for pulling my manger off the wall, Simon kindly built a steel frame to reinforce it and thus prevented me from committing this constant act of vandalism. I am, after all, a big strong horse with extremely powerful jaws and I didn't mean to cause mayhem.

Nic and Simon were very forward thinking on my behalf and placed steel strips along the wooden fence rails to deter me from windsucking or, at least if I did, they would minimise the damage. I soon realised that steel was nowhere near as tasty as wood and Helen always had the Cribox handy to make me think twice about any windsucking fantasies.

Fast forward to 2015, a date we will come to later in this book but of important relevance to this heartfelt confession.

Finding a livery yard for a horse that windsucks is very hard work and Helen was so lucky when Rae accepted me as a resident in 2015 - when I moved into my still current home. What didn't seem to be an issue at first, as I was enjoying life in a small paddock surrounded by electric fencing, soon became a challenge for me to accept and win. Even now I have a very big spring in my step so 7 years ago it was no great shakes for me to escape from this alleged fortress. It only took one jump!

Until recently Rae has tolerated my bad habits despite the damage that I have caused to her fencing. However, although the girls have done brilliantly to restrict my behaviour by managing it with a combination of electric fences and Cribox, I am ashamed to admit that, on several occasions, I have completely pulled down a 5ft wooden gate.

All of a sudden, everything has become like a competition for me. The recent lack of an electric fencing in combination with ageing fence rails means that, shamefully, I have left an indelible mark on the yard. Humiliatingly for me, I have caused Helen to be in a position where she has to purchase new fence rails and I know how frustrated she must be that I don't seem to be able to stop. I know it is wrong, but I can't help myself. It's like a game – the problem being that I have some uncanny knack of detecting when the electric fence battery is dead. Then it's simply one nil to me! Helen has a full-time job keeping up with charging the battery but, like a mystic psychic, I can touch the white string and decide whether I can grab the fence or get a shock. Clever or what?

I feel for Helen when she has to put up with "tale tellers", anti-windsuckers, who love to report any minor infringement just for the sake of causing trouble. I have noticed that Helen now has an impressive array of tools – drill, claw-hammer, nails, mallet – to be ready to repair any damage before it is reported. It's amazing what some people will do for love.

At least at my age, 24 (as I said before) you couldn't possibly say that I was long in the tooth, quite the reverse if you were to examine my front teeth – well-worn would be more accurate. I wish, sincerely, that I could describe myself as a recovering addict but that is, very sadly, not how it is. I so feel for my gorgeous Helen, whom I adore and cherish so much, but I know that I am unlikely to change now and fully deserve the title she gives me, SUCH A MONKEY.

Let's return to our timeline, while trying my very best to deal with, if not completely overcome, my wood addiction.

CHAPTER 12

TEMPORARY ACCOMODATION

2011 was to be a very different year for me. I remember that it seemed to be a time of multiple holidays, experiencing new places and people, most of whom couldn't help themselves when it came to falling in love with me. My reputation and fan base were already huge, this year simply confirmed my legendary status.

Previously, I have touched on how amazing it was to be owned by such an erudite scientist as Helen. At this time, she was a research associate at Cardiff University investigating a population of stem cells that reside in the cartilage of joints. All that on her plate and yet she still found all that time to look after me. How lucky was I? Although for some years Helen had been working on human therapy, her background (and interest) in equine research led her to exploring a treatment for cartilage damage in horses using the stem cells she had identified in the lab.

All this had a really fascinating effect on my lifestyle. Helen had to travel.

California in March, Arizona in May, Colorado in June and July and Switzerland in September. Those were the days of her life, but she was my carer, what about me? Clearly there had to be a long-term plan, she might be enjoying herself globetrotting, but her main responsibility was still to me.

Not much change was needed when she was away for the shorter trips. I just stayed where I was at Blue House farm under the wonderful care of Nic, the skilful artisan who carried out constant maintenance on my manger. There was a big added bonus at the farm at this time because, although my mate Scruffy had found a new residence, I enjoyed the delights of sharing my field with, not one, but two ginger females and you know what they say about redheads! Fly was my favourite, but her mate wasn't half bad either.

Talk about falling on your feet, when Helen was away for her two longer trips, I went to stay with Jacky Leonard in Shirenewton, near Chepstow. I had been there many times for training sessions and knew Jacky well. I was in no doubt that she was a big fan of mine and that my time with her would be the holiday of a lifetime. I wasn't wrong.

When Helen was in Arizona in May I spent a week at Jacky's but, in the summer, I spent almost three months there. I understood that, when Helen was in Colorado in the summer of 2011, she was working on a project with the world's most famous equine orthopaedic surgeon, Dr. Wayne McIlwraith, and because of the set up there she was able to negotiate the cost of seven weeks full livery for me as part of her expenses. All goes to show just how important I was, and still am, to her – I cannot tell you what a great feeling that is.

To be loved is the most wonderful outcome in anyone's life and, despite all my now well-documented faults, *loved* is what I most certainly am.

I had the most fabulous time at Jacky's. She and her wife, Julie, absolutely adored me – so easy to do – and I was treated like a King. The couple lived in a beautiful stone cottage with fields and stables adjacent to it. Being so special, I, of course, had the best stable in the yard and was spoilt rotten. I lapped up the absolute adulation of these adoring fans, they even endured my windsucking without any drama.

I was clearly having such a fantabulous time with Jacky and Julie that, when Helen returned from her research trip to Colorado, she allowed me to remain on an extended holiday with them for another five weeks at her own expense. I know that she was looking to my own happiness and well-being rather than deciding whether to be rid of me once and for all I am, after all, an impossible soul to get out of anyone's system.

.oOo.

During that wonderful time at the stone cottage, not only did Jacky and Julie look after me but also Jacky took on the job of riding me and, with incredible belief and devotion, attempted to continue my dressage training, a bit of a forlorn task. I really liked Jacky -she was such a kind and forgiving rider and was extraordinarily tolerant of my quirky ways. However, it was blindingly obvious that she too was becoming frustrated with my abysmal lack of progress.

So much so that she decided to introduce me to her good friend and physiotherapist Karen Fuller who would be able to give me a thorough once over to find out if I had any deep-rooted problems. Karen did, in fact, unearth a number of minor issues that might have been affecting my progress but, in all honesty, the remedies simply helped my comfort and aches and pains rather than provided the miracle cure for my rather underwhelming dressage career.

Frankly, I very quickly learnt that I could pretend that my muscles were sore so that I could get a lovely, soothing massage from my "Auntie Karen", an ardent fan who adores me to this very day and still visits me regularly. Looking forward to my next massage, Karen.

We got back to normal at Blue House Farm in September of 2011, but before that, on one of her visits to see me at Jacky's, Helen and I met our life-long friends, of whom much more is to be told, Alana and Red. Alana was a similar age to Helen and the two of them hit it off straight away, so lovely to see from my point of view. Alana had, herself, recently acquired a ginger ex-racer called Red. She had stabled Red with Jacky and it was evident that she and Helen had an awful lot in common.

Red is a few inches taller than me and a few years younger. A whipper-snapper at the age of 20. His Racing name was Hang Time, and he was owned by the famous JP McManus and trained by Jessica Harrington in Ireland. His racing career was the total opposite to mine. He had one race. One race! Beaten 107+ lengths in a Maiden Hurdle at Fairyhouse in July 2007 and that was the end of his racing career. I was a serial winner and grandson of Nijinsky – no comparison. Although, legs up, I must admit that Red has never caused Alana as much trouble as I have caused Helen -at least I'm not boring and had an illustrious racing career.

.oOo.

While I was still staying with Jacky, Helen used to visit and meet up with Alana to take me and Red out hacking together. They would build a few small jumps in a field for us to challenge ourselves over and we really did have great fun. I loved all this and, at half my age in those days, I enjoyed approaching the jumps as fast as I could. It was such a buzz. I remember on one such occasion when Julie was watching us zooming about, she had to turn around and return to the house claiming that she needed smelling salts to watch me jump. I must say that the speed at which I approached my fences at that time was definitely not for the faint hearted. Just shows how courageous Helen was too, added to all her other unbelievable qualities.

At this time Jacky was also helping Alana and Red with their dressage and I must admit that Red had much more of an aptitude for this discipline than I did. He was far more laid back and obliging than me and very much looked the part. During the August of 2011 the four of us took part in quite a few dressage competitions and, I seem to remember, we even brought home a trophy on one occasion. I have to admit that the competition wasn't very hot a that event, but a win is a win.

Not all these outings were quite as successful, though. At Usk Agricultural Show, I regressed to type and broke away from the horse trailer and did several laps of the car park prior to our competition classes. I suppose the next fact would be obvious to many, but I can't get my head around it – I just did not perform very well on grass (I suppose you could say that for all surfaces). Helen said that I found grass too exciting and that I managed to keep my head much more together on a synthetic surface.

Still, whether we did badly or reasonably well, we really enjoyed outings with great friends like these and it was so rewarding to have their support. I am so happy to assert that both Alana and Jacky were a tremendous encouragement to Helen and the fact that they kept believing in me was simply wonderful.

If I say so myself, I know just how handsome I looked at these events – I spruce up pretty well you know. Even when I didn't quite put my best hoof forward, I certainly knew that I would catch the eye of many a spectator. Without any conceivable doubt, I have the "je ne sais quoi" of attraction.

When Helen got me back to Blue House Farm at the end of that September, I heard on the grapevine that she been riding a horse called

Teddy in Colorado, by all accounts he looked a bit like me but with the most trainable of personalities. I gleaned that she had a great deal of affection for Teddy.

I pretended that I hadn't missed Helen when she was on her travels. In reality - my God was I jealous!

CHAPTER 13

FANTASTIC TIMES

By the time that 2012 had swung into action, I had an inkling that Helen was becoming more than a little frustrated with the progress or lack of it that I was making on this prickly dressage project. Secretly, most pleasing to me was the decision that she made with regard to this discipline in early January of that year, namely to abandon it altogether for the moment. I was fully aware that Helen was really disappointed that she kept hitting a solid brick wall with me despite all of her efforts but, being perfectly honest, I did try extremely hard to please her but dressage just wasn't my thing.

I knew that giving dressage a break would be good for Helen's mental health, as well as mine, but I also knew that she would definitely try it all again at some time in the future. I know that we are both cut from the same cloth; so very much alike.

For myself, I was very pleased indeed with the giant strides forward that I was making with my jumping ability. I had been ticking along very nicely for some time and I knew that I was beginning to impress Helen, at least in this sphere.

However, I absolutely knew from her touch when she was riding me that, quite often, she wasn't, shall we say, and justifiably so, the most confident. Definitely, I knew that she had the constant fear that I would duck out of a jump at the last instant and that she would end up with a face full of sand or mud. I'd have thought that that was very much part of the fun, well it was for me. I just loved keeping her guessing.

Anyway, it was at this time that Helen decided to enrol us at Usk Riding Club, a great decision because it so helped us to get out and about and gain more experience in just about everything. The club engaged in every horse activity you could think of and ran small competitions to give all the horses and riders targets to aim for. I remember that our first competition for jumping came not long after the imposed moratorium on dressage, at the end of January 2012. The competition was held at Usk College and what a day it was.

Neither of us had any expectations whatsoever and that probably removed any nerves that we both had as we proceeded to jump some, in my view, quite small courses. Would you believe it, we came away with 3 clear rounds that day and a big smile on both our faces. We even had it in us that day to prove our affection for our friends, you will remember from earlier in this story, Alana and Red.

The very handsome Red certainly looked the part in the dressage ring but, most certainly, he couldn't match my confidence when it came to jumping. You see, some show jumps are very simple, just poles and wings, but others have "fillers" underneath the poles. These fillers come in a variety of colours and may even have images or patterns on them. These can be very disconcerting for those horses with, shall we call it, a fragile temperament. That is definitely not me.

At Usk, that day. the course seemed to be saturated with all kinds of these such 'terrifying' obstacles but they mattered not a jot to me as my clear round successes illustrated. Red, however, had major issues on that day at Usk and was proving to be a most uncooperative problem for Alana. Red's problem was that monsters resided in the fillers and why would he have any desire whatsoever to go anywhere near them. Luckily for our firm friends I, well Helen really I suppose, decided to step in to help. We got Alana and Red to follow us onto the course and then, successfully, I led Red around all of the obstacles so that, triumphantly, he could complete his round. Just like Helen and myself, this good deed enabled our special friends to return home feeling fulfilled in their accomplishments. I must say the satisfaction was enormous.

Would you believe it, despite not being really quite ready, we even ended up on the Usk Riding Club Show Jumping Team that spring. It must be said that we didn't trouble the main contenders, but it was still good fun.

Helen stuck to her resolution about the dressage ban and we carried on happily with various trainers and at different venues, popping along to quite a few little competitions and even bringing home a rosette or two in the process.

We also put a bit of time and effort into our cross-country training and, most fortuitously for Helen, we didn't alight upon anything similar to the porta loos that had proved so upsetting to me previously. And here's me castigating Red for being scared of a few coloured shapes – double standards?

I think, in hindsight, that Helen may have regretted not getting into eventing in a more serious way but I also know why she made that decision. True eventing is dressage with a separate show jumping and cross-country course. Of course, we all know by now that dressage is my nemesis. However, the thing about "eventers training" competitions were that they didn't have any dressage included and that the jumping was a combination of show jumps and imitation cross-country jumps, usually all indoors. I couldn't quite believe it but they even had fake water trays.

Helen took me to quite a few of these competitions throughout 2012 and, if I say so myself, we had a great deal of success. I was full of so much confidence now and was ready to take on anything. I was getting bolder and bolder, and it was me that was the driving force in our partnership, compelling Helen to move out of her comfort zone and become totally undaunted and brave. Such a fantastic feeling of unity.

.oOo.

Although I now felt "King of the Jumps", I have to admit that my temperament in the show ring was, at best, unpredictable. After all, going around looking pretty wasn't really my nosebag and, as I often heard Helen remark, it wasn't very exciting for either her or me. To be honest, that is the reason I quite enjoyed misbehaving; it seemed very worthwhile adding a bit of *oomph* to those somewhat staid proceedings. After all, I had, in my initial years in this set, already earned, shall we say, an interesting reputation and one simply had to keep up appearances.

Helen was clearly delighted when the Retraining of Racehorses (RoR) organisation introduced "The Retrained Racehorse Challenge" competition. This was different from the showing classes where the horse walked, trotted and cantered around a ring looking pretty and, hopefully, behaved well. In this competition the horse had to jump a course of rustic show jumps (known to the knowledgeable equestrian as *Working Hunter* fences) as part of the class.

The RoR ran a series of these competitions throughout the year at various venues around the UK, giving every horse the chance to qualify for the final at Royal Windsor the following spring. Now that was something to get the heart thumping, especially for a former racing star like myself. This event was held in August 2012 at The David Broome Event Centre.

I knew that something special was on the cards because of the amount of really serious practising that Helen was putting me through. The practising was fun and I thoroughly enjoyed it because I could actually feel the progress that I was making. Yet, through the vibes of the saddle, I could tell that Helen was a bit nervous. I just knew that whatever was coming up really meant a lot to her. As we travelled to the venue, I was in no doubt that I absolutely had to perform.

Helen had brought her faithful friend, Alana, along to act as my groom and make sure that both myself, and indeed Helen, looked as smart as possible. This involved a great deal of meticulous spa like treatments, the most challenging feat being to ensure that the white socks on my legs were Persil-white.

While Alana was feverishly working at making me even more handsome than I already was, I sneaked a peek at Helen as she walked the course. My empathy with this marvellous woman meant that I knew immediately that nerves were overwhelming her whole persona. My whole being seemed to be in total sync with her thoughts. Automatically, I knew that the jumps were bigger than she expected and that she was questioning herself about the wisdom of taking on this challenge.

I had to be strong with her, take charge, ooze confidence and banish any doubts that were upsetting her. I so wanted to be the horse she dreamed of and I am sure my demeanour and attitude that day gave Helen the positive thoughts that she needed to gain both success and enjoyment.

The format of this competition meant that each competitor had to enter the ring in turn and proceed to jump the course of fences. That all seems pretty straightforward seeing as we had done loads of practice over some nice little fences on our own and in our own space. However, jumping these more daunting obstacles in a large grass ring with people watching was a whole different story and a very tough challenge. Through the reins, I could feel the nervous anticipation in Helen's touch but I had my proper head on today and my thoughts returned to my racing days at Southwell when hundreds of spectators were screaming at me.

Wow! We managed to get round the course with only a single pole down. A relief and a triumph. What next? Something, I fear, that Helen had not anticipated despite all her meticulous preparation.

Once all of us competitors had completed our jumping rounds, we were all asked to come back into the ring at the same time. Now, my record at shows when participating in group activities was where the legend of Kumakawa came into being. I tried my best to concentrate on the job in hand, but the fun definitely started now. When we had all duly assembled in the ring, 12 ex racehorses grouped together like on the start line, sparks would surely begin to fly. Our riders were then asked to instruct us to walk, trot, canter and perform a short gallop, not individually but all at the same time. Crazy!

The judge shouted out what discipline of pace we should be in and it was up to each horse and rider to duly oblige. Unfortunately, I got my wires a little crossed at this moment. You see that many ex-racehorses moving at speed collectively on grass is rather an exciting event. It certainly was for me, like old times, I loved it, but a bit too much. As we moved through the gears, building up speed everybody was doing really well at following the instructions, duly obliging to the changes called. I think that the expression "unbridled pleasure" probably describes my then state of mind, it was completely blown. Whilst all the other competitors had throttled back to a trot, Helen and I were still cantering, sideways. At least I stood out as a competitor.

Once we had got all that nonsense out of the way, we moved on to the next stage of the event which involved all 12 of us standing in a line before being asked to come forward one by one to be given a once over and a third degree by the judges. It was all a bit like a Miss World Pageant, and I was waiting to hear Helen say that all she wanted was "world peace".

Anyway, the judge's job was to examine each horse's conformation and condition, like at Cruft's, and then to find out their age and a bit about their racing career. Of course, Helen had to be forthcoming with all those details and when she announced that I had run in 117 races, judges and spectators alike were completely shocked and stunned. She didn't even tell them that I held the record for the number of races run in during one calendar year. On we went to the final parts of the competition and looked forward to finding out how well, or not, we had done.

I have got to tell you that the judge really rated how I looked and was mightily impressed with my conformation. He was also very complimentary about my jumping ability, something which pleased me immensely. Sadly, however, by this point I had become a bit of a sweaty mess because of my over exertion during the group activity in the ring. My gorgeous plaits, lovingly woven by the equally gorgeous Alana, were starting to fall apart and I was no longer as clean and shiny as when I first entered the ring.

After the rider chat with the judges, the final part of the event involved us entering the ring again, this time on our own, and performing the walk, trot and canter in order to demonstrate my paces and show how well schooled I was. I must admit that I did look a bit ragged by now but, despite that and the fact that I was shattered, my head was back on and I did this last part really well and behaved impeccably. I knew that Helen was proud of me and that meant everything to me.

Once all the competitors had completed this final exercise, we were then asked to walk a large circle around the judges where they called the winners. I really enjoyed that bit.

Both Helen and myself were thrilled when we placed 6th. This in our very first RoR Retrained Racehorse Challenge.

I gathered that the feedback from the judge was that, if I had behaved myself in the group event, we would have placed much higher up. Not my fault that I was the best racehorse there!

CHAPTER 14

A MAGICAL WEEKEND

Almost from the very moment that I arrived in South Wales and completed my transfer from Ross and Karen, Helen had become heavily involved in (the now disbanded) Ex Racers Club. Indeed, throughout the first eight months of this 2012, she had become one of the prime movers in organising The Ex Racers Championship Show which was to be held at Milton Keynes. I knew that this project had taken up a lot of Helen's time and I really don't know how she fitted everything in. Show, work, me.

This time all her efforts were concentrated on organising the schedule, judges and sponsors etc. I knew that I hadn't qualified for this prestigious championship and thus had been spared all that practising. What concerned me, however, was what to become of me when Helen was away for those few days. It appeared to me that no one had been put on standby to see to my needs and, of course, it was then that I realised just how important Helen was to me, always putting my health and happiness first. Yes, it struck home, I was a 24 hour, 365 days a year responsibility.

Imagine my joy when I realised that my wonderful owner couldn't bear to be without me for those few days. It turned out that there was no way that she was leaving me at home this time, despite the long trip to Milton Keynes. I suspected that she wouldn't be able to resist getting me to take part in some of the off-piste competitions, but they were just fun and games.

So, on the morning of Friday 29th September 2012, we set off on our 140 mile trip to Milton Keynes Equestrian Centre. Actually, I couldn't quite believe that it was just the two of us making the trip. I was a notorious handful, after all, and Helen usually got one of her good friends to come along and help. I decided to do my utmost to be a model gentleman this time. At least I had no competition pressure to weigh me down.

Our horsebox was one of the first to arrive that Friday afternoon, so Helen was able to unload me and settle me in to my temporary stable without any fuss and bother. I watched, fascinated, as one by one our fellow ex racehorses arrived, the owners settling in their horses and pitching their tents. Did I know any of the horses? Had I raced against any of them? Beaten them, of course.

We were all extremely lucky that it was not too cold that night, although Helen managed to get a space in a caravan – organiser's privilege I suspect. What was very special, though, was that the caravan was right next to my bivouac. It was lovely to be sleeping so close to Helen each night.

I know that Helen has made a lot of lifelong friends through the Ex Racers-Club and up to that competition she hadn't actually met many of them in person. From the perfect position of my stable, it was a great feeling to see the interaction between all these people and animals and I knew what a wonderful experience it was for Helen to meet all them and their horses face to face.

I so enjoyed watching and listening as she mingled with her friends and fellow organisers, Cala, Emma, Sarah, Kerrie, Denise and Alex. I heard Helen thank the group for all the remarkable effort that they had put into the club and organising that championship weekend. She topped it off by adding that she wouldn't have made the long trip, with me in tow, if it wasn't for all of them. A terrific thank you, I thought.

Giving myself a very big pat on the back, I must add that probably the most remarkable thing about this whole weekend was how well behaved I was. The vibes were good for me from the word go. I was in likeminded company; I didn't know many of the horses but we all immediately became mates. An amazing aura seemed to permeate the whole event. There wasn't a single point in the entire weekend where I even felt like being naughty or stressy. So unlike me – and a nice enjoyable change for everyone.

Completely out of the blue, on the Saturday, Helen decided to break our dressage ban. I said I knew that something like this would happen! We competed in the dressage competition – no practice, off the cuff, spur of the moment. No time for pent up worries. Do you know, we did quite well and thoroughly enjoyed ourselves. We were on a roll. We then had great fun later in the day when she put me into the show jumping arena. Then, joy upon joy, I noticed that Ross and Karen had come along to visit me. It turned out that Helen had told them that we would be at Milton Keynes that weekend and that was only about 50 miles from their house. I knew they wouldn't miss the chance of visiting me, let alone have the chance to watch me jump.

Everything was brilliant that day. The atmosphere was just fantastic, and the day had the perfect ending when Helen won the pairs jumping when riding my old mate (and lookalike) Scooby (aka Knightsbridge King). She was absolutely thrilled with that. I slept really well that night, dreaming of being a dressage champion.

After all the fun and frolics of the Saturday, for Helen Sunday was the serious day and the main purpose of the weekend. Horses came from far and wide to compete in the numerous classes and battle for the championship. I knew that Helen would be rushed off her feet with the serious amount of organising that needed to be done and now she was entering me for some of the non-championship classes as well. Was she mad? I knew that I had to behave especially well. This was my big chance to say thank you, I wasn't going to mess it up.

When I think back, I was unbelievably cooperative that day. Helen was running around making sure things ran smoothly while at the same time competing with me in different classes. I stayed super cool and laid back. I knew that nothing was expected of me there. So there was no reason for me to feel under pressure – and I just went with the flow. As a result, incredible things happened.

All these years later, I am still in a state of shock at what transpired on that Sunday afternoon. Such a shame that Ross and Karen could only come for the Saturday because it was like the good old days of my racing career – picking up trophies and posing for photographs.

On that Sunday, not only did I cope with all the madness of the organisational shenanigans, but I did an amazing job in masquerading as a proper show pony and won two classes. The first class I won was the *In-Hand Class* and deservedly so, if I say so myself. Rarely have I looked so amazing. All to do with serenity, I think, as was my absolutely impeccable behaviour.

The second class I won - and to this day I really don't know how I managed it - was the *Best Riding Club Horse*. I think that I was just "in the zone" - relaxed, confident, and at peace with the world. On this day, I just knew that going round the ring with many other ex-racehorses and jumping a small fence as part of the routine was neither stressful nor over-exciting. I couldn't have done it better. It was the performance of a lifetime, and I loved every second of it. A beautiful exhibition, poetry in motion.

More to the point, Helen was overcome with pride and joy. She even shed a tear when we were handed our red ribbon and trophy by the judge.

Glory upon glory, not only did we win those two classes, but we were also presented with a trophy for the horse and rider that had attained the most points throughout the weekend. Unbelievable.

Truly, we were amazing that weekend and we drove the long trip home with a clutch of trophies and rosettes, exhausted but very, very happy. We both felt like superstars.

This was a weekend of fun, laughter and (happy) tears.
Magical. An everlasting memory.

So happy to be cominig home with ribbons!

CHAPTER 15

FAREWELL TO MY GORGEOUS LEAH

As the new page on the calendar revealed the year 2013, considerable trepidation filled my heart as this was a year marked by that most ominous and significant number in my life – 13. Along with my previous owner, Karen, the alignment of the number 13 quite often meant that good things would happen but, equally, it was regularly the precursor of sad and unhappy events.

Which way would the coin fall this time?

Indeed, in this year of 13, things started so badly that I look back with guilt about the terrifying expense that I caused Helen by so many, and some unnecessary, accidents and incidents. The very first event occurred just as we entered this year. This time it was a quite severe leg injury which, to be absolutely honest, seemed to appear from nowhere. One moment I was having a great time frolicking with Leah, the next minute I had lots of blood pouring from a gaping wound on my leg.

Poor Helen was in a state of shock when she saw it and I imagined she thought, "This is just typical of Kuma. How on earth has he managed to do that? It must take some super horsey imagination to create all these problems." I refused to imagine her thoughts about the incoming vet's bill – too embarrassing, even for me!

As I continued my latest convalescence, wonder upon wonder, the snow arrived. I love the snow - the look of it, the feel of it and the joy that it seems to bring to everybody, especially the children.

At this time, quite a few owners in the yard had small children and they all loved visiting the stables and petting all of us. The snowy conditions, combined with the picturesque mountain scenery, created the perfect setting for them to let themselves go and have some serious fun. This season's heavy snowfall had created the conditions for making fantastic large snow sculptures.

The children found it highly amusing to build an extremely large snow woman, a most unusual and curious creation. Of course, I couldn't resist the opportunity to investigate this strange and imposing addition to the yard.

As I tried my best to satisfy my curiosity and work out the nature of this snow object, all of the owners took the chance to capitalise on such an amazing photo opportunity and I was, yet again, sealed into immortality by many cameras. This was a real competition composition – horse and snow woman. What else would you need to get into the Countryfile calendar?

Me and the snow woman

Me and Leah

It was during these early weeks of 2013 that I learned that Helen was about to fly off to San Antonio in Texas for another one of her very important scientific conferences, though my own view was that she just wanted to escape the vagaries of the British winter. However, in all seriousness, I knew full well how emotionally torn she was about making this trip. Not only did she have me to worry about but, at this very difficult time, she also was most concerned about the health of her, and my, lovely Leah.

For as long as I could remember, Leah had been my rock, my steadfast friend and devoted guardian. We did everything together. Although all collie dogs are amazing, Leah really was extra, extra special. A truly loyal and loving friend. Helen had not had Leah all the way from puppyhood and, consequently, was unaware of her exact age. However, we all surmised that she was about 15 years old which, strange to say, was exactly the same age as me at this time.

Justifiably, Helen was right to be extremely worried about Leah because 15 is quite a good age for a collie to achieve. At this juncture in her life, she was experiencing a great deal of difficulty with her back legs which would often give way under her. Also, most unpleasantly for her, she tended to be doubly incontinent at night. With all these problems on her mind, Helen made absolutely sure that we were both in the safe hands of her most trusted friends at the yard before completing the arrangements for the journey to San Antonio. She made sure that she would receive daily reports on our well-being while she was away and, although her time away gave her an extremely stressful seven days, the fact that she knew we were both in the safest of hands helped in giving her a relatively worry-free trip. It goes without saying that she was more than delighted that we were both well on her return.

It was heart breaking for me to watch the decline in Leah's wellbeing during late February and March 2013 and I knew that things were not boding well. I had an incredibly deep connection with my wonderful Leah and we had symbiotic relationship. Sadly, on her last visit to the actual yard, I had the desperate feeling that this would be the last time I would see Leah and, devastatingly, two days after this distraught final farewell on Wednesday 10th April 2013 Leah passed away. Helen was desolate and I just could not believe it. For weeks after this tumultuous event, I kept looking for Leah every time Helen arrived at the yard. It is so very upsetting, even now, to describe the gaping hole that Leah left in my heart when she died. She was always by my side and went everywhere with us. I believe she always will be.

CHAPTER 16

CAR TROUBLE

As winter turned into spring, physically I could feel the distress of Helen as she struggled to deal with the loss of Leah. I knew that she was having difficulty coping with such a silence around the house and I was aware that it was up to me to do my very best to try to fill the massive hole that had been left in both of our lives. I did my utmost to inject some fun into proceedings by being extra boisterous in order to provide Helen with a little bit of distraction from her deepest mournful thoughts. I believe that Helen appreciated these efforts and, in fact, it cemented the bond, if indeed cement was needed, between us. We continued our training, this time combining show jumping with the dressage, and we managed to get out and about in the lanes, gaining the confidence and desire to start competing again in late April of this 2013.

With all the competitions and shows that Helen perpetually entered us into, mobility was obviously a major issue. Good transport was one of the main ingredients that success was based on. If you weren't there, you couldn't compete.

Although an amazing brainbox and at the very top of her profession, Helen was not especially good with or about motor vehicles. We had been travelling with the help of her Land Rover Discovery Mk2 for as long as I could remember and it was definitely having major issues. In May of that year, it quite simply stopped. Without any warning whatsoever, as Helen was bombing down the dual carriageway near the yard, the turbo blew up and caused an horrendous trail of black smoke behind her. Of course, she denied all responsibility for this incident and actually confided in me that she would be forever grateful that she, for once, didn't have me in the trailer behind her on that occasion. I was well pleased. Hours at the roadside waiting for assistance would not have been my idea of fun, especially with all that traffic whizzing by.

The poor Land Rover was written off and it was clear that the prospect of getting me mobile again was weighing heavily on Helen's shoulders. This somewhat daunting problem was exacerbated by the fact that Helen, despite being a lover of Land Rovers, was now put off them by countless friends who told her in no uncertain manner to steer clear of the brand because her experience was just the latest in a series of incidents which had trashed the reputation of this particular make of vehicle. Responding to this negative information Helen sped past many Land Rover dealerships as she ventured on her new car buying expedition.

The result of many sustained weekends of car hunting came to an abrupt conclusion with the decision to purchase a rather snazzy, royal blue VW Touareg - 8 years old and affordable. After a good-few weeks off, I was just as delighted as Helen to get back on the competition road again. The excitement was palpable as I clambered aboard the trailer ready for the short journey to a local riding club event. Out on the road again, just a week after the purchase of our new super motor.

However, as Helen turned the corner to get out of the yard and, having travelled barely 100 metres, our plans were thwarted. As we entered the initial slight incline preceding the mountain road, the engine cut out. Helen, with an outstanding flash of inspiration, decided to see what happened to the Touareg when it had nothing to tow. She decoupled the trailer and gave the snazzy VW another try. No problem. To cut a long story short, each time she hitched up the trailer and tried to go up the hill, the engine cut out. Every single time. I felt so guilty. Without me, no problem, with me, impossible. Helen was the very definition of frustration, with much descriptive vocabulary accompanied by some interesting, indeed weird, physical movements illustrating the same. Abject despair and failure.

To make matters worse, Volkswagen had no clue as what was causing the problem though, even as a horse, I could dare to reason that the engine simply wasn't up to it. The upshot at the time was that the company took the vehicle away for evaluation, causing our training and my progress to be severely interfered with, in effect putting everything we were trying to achieve on hold. How many trophies might I have won if the car had only been up to the job?

In the end, putting everybody out of their misery, Helen received a full refund and, in utter desperation, purchased a 9-year-old LPG converted black Range Rover V8. Hindsight is, of course, a wonderful thing, although some might say "If you are in possession of all the facts, isn't it utter stupidity to repeat a mistake?" But here was Helen riding straight back down that same track. The Range Rover blew its head gasket within a few months. I was side lined yet again!

CHAPTER 17

DAISY, JOYBRINGER.

The 13 in the year was proving to be a very ill omen indeed. We were in dire need of some good things to happen. I could feel through my whole body and persona just how frustrated and depressed Helen was. Bad things had become routine and the element of fun, so important to a constantly stressed high flier like Helen, had almost totally vanished from her life.

She had had to endure the monumental loss of Leah, my mishaps and so many costly experiences and disasters with vehicles, while her main avenue of joy and release had been closed off to her because we were so severely restricted to activities in and around the confines of the yard. No competitions meant no naughtiness and, if I have the nerve to say so myself, my naughtiness was desperately missed. My entertaining behaviour was a reason to get up in the morning. Mischievous Kumakawa was a great therapeutic remedy that sorely was being missed in Helen's life. The pressure was definitely on me to be a source of joy for my wonderful owner and, looking back, I can only hope that the little things I did to tickle her helped her through those very dark times.

Along came Helen's 38th birthday - 7th July 2013. Surely, at last, something great and special would come along to brighten our lives. As it happened, we couldn't have asked for more.

A birthday treat meant that Helen was invited to view a litter of border collie puppies who had been reared a little way away near Swansea. On that happy birthday morning, Helen met and instantly fell in love with a most beautiful border collie puppy. She brought home Daisy that very same day.

So much despair turned into unbridled joy and when, only two days later, Helen introduced Daisy to me, I fell in love with her immediately and absolutely knew that she would heal our very happy family.

I have never been so right.

Daisy – The day Helen brought her home

The very moment Daisy first clapped eyes on me

Daisy watching me at The Hand Equestrian Centre.

We had that same telepathic empathy which I experienced with Leah. It was uncannily like a reincarnation and we both knew that forever we would be soulmates. Like Leah, Daisy travels everywhere with Helen and me, wherever and whenever we go, she is always there. She guards and mothers me in the yard and is as much an angel for me as Helen. I am definitely a two-woman horse and I love it.

Just five days after Daisy arrived, this incredible puppy attended her very first horse show at the David Broome Centre. It was only 12th July and yet she made the most amazing debut you could imagine. No superlative is adequate for this amazing puppy.

While Helen and I were competing in the arena, Daisy was paraded around all the other show rings by her instant and adoring fans. It was, quite simply, impossible not to fall in love with her. She took to the horse scene like a duck to water and has been right by our side ever since.

If ever the number 13 was lucky, this was, certainly, the time.

I don't know whether you'd call it an advantage or a disadvantage when a collie puppy gets to know you inside out, seemingly instantaneously, from the very first moment that you meet. Unquestionably, within those first few special moments, Daisy had me completely pegged. She, probably correctly, believed that she could tell me exactly what to do. That superhero border collie spirit was fully embedded in her DNA right down to the tips of her toes.

A very early display of this power of control came at The Hand Equestrian centre in early August of this year. Remember, Daisy was still only weeks old. Helen had entered me into an event where we were required to perform both a dressage test and a show jumping round. The combined score of the two events would count as the result. What happened at this event cannot be embellished upon because the whole thing was caught on camera and can, I assure you be fully verified.

This time I was upstaged as the star of the show by this talented and simply brilliant puppy. As I was actually engaged in performing one of my more superior show jumping rounds, Daisy ran into the arena and followed me and Helen round the whole course, jumps and all. The ecstatic spectators rose as one to hail this astounding extra entertainment. Priceless!

The beginning of a long and devoted relationship on all three of our parts. Daisy has proved to be the most honourable heiress to the fabulous Leah. It has been a real and enduring joy to have been associated with these two most special of dogs.

CHAPTER 18

STILL A NAUGHTY BOY

After a life littered with misdemeanours since joining Helen in 2007, you might possibly think that I would have learned a very great deal about all the horsey things that I have been taught. Indeed, I have taken an awful lot on board but the total processing of all these elements has, somehow, remained beyond me. It is a real conundrum as to why I hadn't driven Helen completely crazy, even after those initial five years. What state her mental health must be in now, all these years later, I dread to think.

Sometimes I just couldn't seem to cope with the environment I was placed in. So often, it seemed that I was a square peg in a round hole; I could only try my best and I always did.

In the middle of August, that 2013, Helen had entered me in another combined show jumping and dressage event, this time at Chepstow racecourse – most prestigious. However, that word "racecourse" might give you an inkling of what possibly might be about to happen. At this moment, I will state categorically that Helen must have realised pretty quickly, though still far, far too late, that she most definitely should have known better.

Despite it not being a race day, the sight of the iconic racecourse white railings, combined with the all-pervasive atmosphere of the show, was enough to flick that "racing switch" in my head. Exciting memories flooded back into my subconscious and I became totally confused as to what was expected of me.

With all her supreme riding skills, Helen managed to get us through the dressage test but, by the time we got to the show jumping discipline, it was all becoming a bit (or a lot) of a blur for me. Confusion reigned and, suddenly, I didn't know if I was show jumping or racing.

Me at Chepstow

Quite clearly, my speed indicated that I was still an extremely talented racehorse but, on this occasion, I behaved like one of those horses who break free at the stalls and then run around the track for ages before being caught. The term is, I believe, "boiled over". Everything became a bit too much for me and I needed to escape. In utter disgrace, after this latest infamous show stopping performance, I was returned to the trailer to cool down before the miserable journey back home.

Helen, however, following on from all that excitement that I had provided her with in the show ring, desperately needed to unwind a little bit before taking on that drive. As I stood on the naughty step in the trailer, I watched remorsefully as Helen went for a walk around all the show tents with Daisy by her side. Purely by chance, she discovered that one of these tents featured "show classes for dogs". What a result. On the spur of the moment, our esteemed and intrepid owner entered Daisy for the "best puppy" class and, in spite of being the youngest puppy at just fourteen weeks old and never having had any show experience whatsoever, she performed with amazing aplomb and was placed 4th. What an incredible feat in her very first and completely unplanned attempt at competing. I was so proud that you could see the glow emanating from the trailer.

So it was that in spite of me, unwittingly it must be stressed, doing my very best to sabotage the whole day, Daisy came to the rescue and we didn't go home empty handed. In fact, we all felt very accomplished and, of course, I could claim credit for being the instigator of Daisy's first impromptu success.

Told you that we were linked telepathically.

Helen hugging Daisy after being placed 4th in the best puppy class at Chepstow show

.oOo.

After Daisy's astounding success at Chepstow, the pressure was now on me to gain some serious rosettes. I had a legendary reputation for all the wrong reasons and it was time to put that right. Fair play to Helen, she has so much faith in me and was always my biggest fan. She looks on me as having true ability, and worthy of competing at the highest level. To her, I am not just another reality star.

Because of her absolute belief in me, Helen decided that we should have another bash at the Retraining of Racehorses (ROR) challenge at The Wales and West Hunter Show. This was the event that we placed 6th at in 2012. This time I delivered. I showed incredible improvement in each and every discipline. The serious competition of the Daisy factor most definitely concentrated my mind and made my want to experience some of the glory she had already basked in in her short life. Having Daisy's positive vibes alongside me certainly added to my self-belief and I couldn't help but rack up the points. The fact that I was so much better than before in all the elements of the test resulted in me finishing 2nd.

Helen was ecstatic and I didn't feel half bad myself. This was a spectacular achievement for me, and I didn't know whether to be more proud or slightly disappointed when I overheard the head judge tell Helen that, definitely, I would have come first if I had not let myself down yet again in the "group go-round" part of the class, my Achilles heel. I have always struggled with that particular part of the class in shows, it is so much like a race to me and, remember, I won a lot of my races. I could always win races when I fancied it.

This quite amazing placing in a top show actually meant that I had qualified for the national final of this event at The Royal Windsor Horse Show in the following spring, 2014. However, there was not a single doubt in my mind that Helen would entertain even the most fleeting thought about me going there to compete. She was, quite correctly, well aware that I would never be able to cope with the atmosphere at such a large show, let alone accepting that the size of the obstacles that would be needed to be jumped in such a prestigious final would be far too much for me. The fervent atmosphere at a top horse show is unrelenting and continuous whereas, when you are racing, the punters are screaming at you for two minutes. I know my limitations.

I was really pleased that the implausibility of Helen appearing at The Royal Windsor Horse Show did not detract for one moment from this success. On the plus-side, I knew that, from a very young age, it had always been Helen's dream for her name to appear in the famous Horse and Hound Magazine and, by dint of my 2nd place here, at this most prestigious event, finally she achieved that dream.

RoR Challenge August 2013

14th August - **BEAUFORT HUNT SUPPORTERS SHOW, Gloucestershire**
Results: 1st JUMPTY DUMPTY - Renee Tuck; 2nd RIVERTOWN - Anna Layton; 3rd WAD
Julian Minchen
20th August* - **WALES & WEST HUNTER SHOW, Wales**
Results: 1st MONTANEL - Mandy Owen; 2nd KUMAKAWA - Helen McCarthy; 3rd FREED
Follett; 4th DISTANT PROSPECT - Claire Chambers
21st August* - **VALE OF GLAMORGAN, Wales**
Results: 1st SHERKHAN - Rachel Thomas; 2nd BUCKINGHAM BOYS - Clare Poole; 3rd I
Mortimer; 4th QUO VIDEO - Jessica Mills

Results in the Horse and Hound Magazine!

.oOo.

No doubt I should have spoken earlier in this treatise about Helen's thoughts on me trying eventing. Let's put that right.

Eventing comprises the triple disciplines of dressage, show jumping and cross country. In the last chapter I spoke about how proud I was of the faith that Helen always had in my ability and now, I realise more than ever that she always put my well-being and mental health at the forefront of her desires for me to do well. She must have had reservations about me taking on the challenge of eventing and that it might be all too overwhelming for me. Quite rightly, she must have thought that performing a dressage test on the same day as partaking in a cross-country event was simply asking for trouble. Perhaps, deep down, she wondered if it might be a great idea but, in the cold light of reality, she just wasn't brave enough to take that chance. Until 2013.

Until 2013, when - putting all that doubt behind us – it was the time to have a go. Fresh from achieving legendary, literary status in Horse and Hounds magazine, this just had to be the right time to have another real crack at cross country. Something had just clicked in my brain. I wanted success so badly. I knew I had the talent and now, out of nowhere, I had the self-belief.

An effervescent Helen took me to a number of training sessions at Leyland Court, near Bristol and we tried all different types of obstacles, including water jumps for the first time. Bear in mind that this is me, Kumakawa, the horse that was terrified of getting his feet wet on the beach. Who possibly could believe that I would so enjoy playing in the water on a cross country course?

Helen was so chuffed with me it was embarrassing. What a marvellous time of fun and joy. Everlasting memories.

Cross country training at Leyland Court

Look – Paddling!

CHAPTER 19

NEAR DEATH EXPERIENCE

2013 was displaying, in glorious technicolour, all those things that the number 13 had threatened to exhibit. Sadness, joy, success, failure. With one month left to the end of this extraordinary year, what else had fate in store for us all?

Traditionally, in the horse calendar, either during the last weekend in November or the first weekend in December, The David Broome Event Centre hold a Christmas themed show jumping competition. I believe that in this year that the festivities were in December. So we set off on our journey to the venue with mixed feelings of excitement and trepidation. Would I behave? Would I do well? On this occasion, however, neither of these questions were answered.

What transpired was a blue lighted emergency journey to the veterinary hospital in Gloucester.

We had arrived at the showground in perfect time and, as per usual, Helen parked the car and trailer and went off to walk the course whilst I was quite content to munch on my hay on the trailer - building up my strength for the events later on that day. All of a sudden, I felt terrible, I mean absolutely awful, the worst feeling that I have ever experienced in my life. I completely lost all senses and, to be honest, I hadn't a clue as to what was happening to me. I was totally disorientated and was banging about in the trailer, my balance completely out of sync.

Luckily for me, Helen was, at that very moment, returning from her walkabout and, from some distance could hear the banging and see the trailer rocking from side to side. As she rushed over and opened the door, she discovered me in a very distressed state. I was so fortunate that she is such a level-headed and controlled individual. No panic, just immediate and reasoned evaluation of the situation. To her, there appeared to be no reason for my behaviour. She had left me moments ago happily munching on my hay. I wasn't caught on anything in the trailer but, obviously, I was showing clear signs of pain and distress. Immediately, Helen led me off the trailer, the result of this being that all I wanted to do was to collapse in a heap on the floor. She concluded that I had colic. Do not lay down.

The vet was called without a moments delay and yet it seemed like it took forever, probably longer than that for Helen, for him to arrive. She, herself, was nearing exhaustion from trying to keep me walking and stopping me from falling in a heap on the ground. All I wanted to do was roll around to try and disperse the pain.

The vet's response time was far quicker than it seemed to all of us involved and he immediately went into examination mode and assessed my condition. Certainly, it was serious and after a fair old dose of pain relief he decided to send me to the veterinary hospital post haste. His instructions to the driver, "Do not hang around. This animal must be seen without delay." Hence my "blue light" experience, an experience which simply got me to the emergency services at the veterinary hospital in Gloucester.

Time had just evaporated. It was impossible to pinpoint how long this mayhem had been going on, it was like time was passing in slow motion yet simultaneously was flashing by. The rest of the day was a complete blur of tears and panic for both of us. It is quite obvious that I am nowhere near as clever as Helen and, while she struggled to work out what was best to do, I really didn't know what was happening to me. I just was very aware that things were not very good. I do not know if I was a good, cooperative patient (I certainly hope that I was) but I do know how urgently my case was handled. The staff at the hospital were wonderful to get me through the initial emergency, get me comfortable and put me on the road to recovery.

It turned out that I had been afflicted by a condition called "nephrosplenic entrapment". Now, that's a tricky one even for someone with the tongue twister name like Kumakawa. Apparently "nephro" is derived from the Latin for kidney and "splenic" refers, not unsurprisingly, to the spleen. Basically, it is a type of colic that occurs when the large colon gets entrapped over the nephrosplenic ligament. In a horse, the nephrosplenic ligament connects the left kidney to the spleen. (I know that I sound like some kind of super vet or doctor here, but I'm only copying the diagnosis that the hospital gave to Helen. Cheating a bit but …hey?)

To continue. It is not clear what the cause of such an ailment is. Vets suspect that it is the result of colonic motility dysfunction or an accumulation of gas, which allows the large colon to move between the spleen and the body wall. (I am sure that you will be delighted to have all that information at your fingertips.)

My diagnosis was confirmed after multiple examinations and scans and Helen was given the comfort of being informed that, more often than not, the first line of treatment for this condition was straightforward and non-invasive. Non-surgical treatment is attempted first and this involves the administration of intravenous fluids and painkillers, augmented by copious exercise. The idea behind this treatment being that if you starve a horse, thus deflating the gut, and then exercise the animal, the gut naturally returns to its correct position. All pretty matter of fact really!

Lucky Kumakawa had struck gold yet again. This line of intervention worked for me, but not without some significant side effects. Side effects which not only affected me but also the fantastic people who were trying to help me.

Even now, I find it very hard to believe that during this healing process I became a very, very dangerous animal. If there is one special thing that I love, it is my food. Of course, I was oblivious to the fact that I was being denied food for my own good. I was completely and utterly outraged that I was being starved for days. My answer to this deprivation was to channel my anger into my body and unleash the primitive desire to lunge at any human being that ventured within my vicinity. It is only now that I realise what an absolute monster I became during this treatment period.

When I was about to be discharged as a patient, I can recall the words spoken to Helen by one of the vets: "Do you know that Kumakawa had a warning sign outside his stable instructing staff not to attempt to deal with him alone because of the real danger of being bitten or kicked?" Me? Surely not!

Danger! Beware!

I find it quite amusing now, as I reminisce, that I was deeply concerned at that time because I had indeed turned into the monster from hell.

I was so, so lucky. The treatment worked and it was only a few days before I was discharged from this superb hospital a completely well horse.

By the same token, I am in no doubt whatsoever that the hospital staff were absolutely delighted to see the back of me. That's me, fame and notoriety wherever I go and whatever I do.

I was so pleased to get home to the comforts of my own stable and my own field, able to enjoy the company of all my pals and revel in the incredible mothering of Daisy. It was fantastic to see the release of all that terrible stress from Helen's shoulders. It was a wonderful feeling to realise that someone cared for you that much.

2013 certainly lived up to its billing. In the end you would have to say that it was a great year.

Being Starved in hospital

Back home in my field with a brand-new rug on and a full tummy

CHAPTER 20

WHAT WOULD BECOME OF ME?

It was a fantastic feeling being fit as a fiddle again and, as the clock ticked over into the new year, my mind wandered into the dreamland of wondering what the future months held in store. What field of excellence would Helen decide to steer me into? Would there be an array of rosettes surrounding me or would I have disgraced myself again in some way?

I must say it is quite good fun being in dreamland, it's certainly a lot more pleasant than reality and reality is where we were when it sunk in that this was Helen's last year as a research associate. I overheard her telling a friend at the yard that her grant funding was going to end in September and I could feel that she was very stressed that she would be out of a job when that funding ended.

Hang on a minute, Helen with no job and no income, what would happen to me? Now I was stressed out as much she was, if not more so. The future does not bode well for homeless horses, especially one of my age, although I was much younger then. The prospects of that research continuing after September were slim and so job applications and interviews took over our world. There wasn't much that I could do to help, just be good in the stable and be nice if we went out hacking. It was a worrying time for both of us but I had the solace of knowing just how much fight and determination Helen had and has, in her.

Luckily for me, she secured a lectureship at Cardiff University at the second time of trying and I was ecstatic with joy when I realised that I would be keeping the excellent lifestyle that I had become accustomed to. That's the problem with luxury, when you get used to it, it's very hard to imagine life without it.

Helen's new position meant no more travelling to all those fantastic locations around the world but she did manage to fit in visits to Houston, New Orleans and Davos, in Switzerland. These were the last of her work-related trips, which finally should have meant the end of my visits to babysitters. However, other dramas were unfolding within the yard and my resolutions about being, nice, good and helpful were fast falling about my ears.

When Helen spent time away, I went on my own holidays with Auntie Marina (Marina Evans), who was our instructor at the time. Marina is a real character and I loved her to bits but I'm still not sure how she felt about me. I rather think that all my antics frustrated her, more than a bit. Nevertheless, she was always good for a laugh and I loved her company.

As you may recall from previous chapters, at Blue House Farm, Steve used to help out Helen with me. Steve owned two chestnut mares who were stabled there and Helen would do the morning shift of chores and he would do the afternoon shift. To set the scene on the latest drama, it all related to the fact that, for some unaccountable reason, I have always been an utter nightmare to handle in the field. I cannot work out the cause of this problem, whether something unpleasant happened to me in early life when I was in a similar situation or something like that – the trust is I really don't know.

What I do know is this. Many a time I had Helen shaking with fear as she tried to hold on to me while I was rearing up above her head. I remember, when I first moved in with her, I used to wind her up by planting myself like a rock when she got the headcollar on me. All in fun, you understand. I used to toy with her. My favourite trick was to let her pull on the lead rope to encourage me forward then, without warning I would rear up, strike out with my hooves, pull back suddenly and break free. Helen certainly didn't find it quite as funny as I did, especially when any spectators would fall about laughing as I galloped around the field with my headcollar still in place and my lead rope dangling around my hooves. I honestly was unaware that Helen was really frightened by all this frivolity. I suppose she was terrified about having to catch me again knowing the likelihood that the same sequence of events would happen again and again until I gave in and decided that it was time to come in. Naughty child syndrome really, but great fun nevertheless.

I realised that Helen wouldn't put up with this behaviour forever so I made the most of it while I could. Then she came up with the solution, the Chifney bit and lunge line. The lunge line is about 15 metres long so, if I pulled back on it, Helen had a much better chance of keeping me under control. The length also meant that I would be a lot farther away from her head if I decided to rear up and jump around. Meanwhile, the Chifney is a mouth bit that, shall we say, has anti rearing properties – all very unpleasant for me and that is why I have nothing but full respect for its controlling influences. I have heard from other horses that the Chifney is quite dangerous if used incorrectly and I can well believe it. It certainly had the right effect on me and, without doubt, probably saved Helen's bacon many times.

Come to think of it, I'm pretty sure that the Chifney is used in racing an awful lot. In fact, I probably was the victim of it many times in my racing career. Who knows, it may even have been the source of all my misbehaviour. Only saying!

CHAPTER 21

HE SHOULD HAVE LISTENED

Back to Steve and Blue House Farm. I know that Helen always instructed him to bring me in with a regular bridle and lunge line or the Chifney and lunge line. However, for some godforsaken reason, he more often than not ignored her request and this refusal had serious repercussions in the end. In fact, it eventually led to us leaving Blue House Farm. What Steve didn't realise, unfortunately, was that Helen's request was for his own safety. She knew that, given a piece of string I would unravel it all and that was the tack I took with Steve's carelessness. It was playtime for me but, on this occasion, it was me that got badly hurt.

On 31st January 2014, Steve was bringing me in, casually as per usual. In winter, I am always very keen to get back into my cosy bed and although, when it is cold and wet, I tend not to plant myself and refuse to come in, I know that I am far too keen and far too difficult to hold for the handler. You will probably have witnessed it yourself when a poor stable lad/lass is struggling to hold a fit racehorse as it makes its way around the parade ring and onto the course itself. This was definitely me all over. Coming in at night I would rarely walk, always jog and it was incredibly difficult for anyone to hold onto me without a bridle or a Chifney. On this day, Steve did his usual thing and tried to bring me in with just a headcollar and lead rope. Low and behold, it was so easy to get loose and have some fun. I was so exuberant at putting one over on him that I just let rip and galloped everywhere and anywhere.

Unfortunately, it all backfired dreadfully on me that day. I don't know how or why I was racing around so wildly, but I sustained a really nasty injury on the lowest part of my leg. It was a very deep cut and in such an awkward place that I knew it would be painful for a long time and a difficult wound to heal. Helen didn't know what to say but was clearly very upset at what had happened, especially as she could not, for the life of her, work out how the injury had happened.

Consequently, I was out of action from that February right through until April that year. It sort of reminded me of the enforced layoffs I had when I was racing. Layoffs then were cool though, at my age now, they were boring. Enough said, my recovery this time was lengthy and expensive. It was such a deep cut that took months to improve and, indeed, it still gives me gyp until this very day. Helen owed a tremendous debt of gratitude to her wonderful team of health workers that always seem to be at my disposal, Karen Fuller (physio), David Agnew (vet), and our fabulous farrier, Sam Rooney. By the way, I was extremely grateful and in awe of their treatments as well.

.oOo.

So far, 2014 could have been a rerun for the first half of 2013 what with all the bad luck the pair of us were having. There was the stress of Helen's employment issues, now exacerbated by the expense of my injury that was taking forever to heal and, as the pot of reserve money was rapidly diminishing in size, to add fuel to the fire, the head gasket of Helen's Land Rover blew in the June. This was the same car that she had bought 12 months earlier. It was 10 years old and LPG converted which had been great for fuel costs but, and you know what I am going to say, not cheap to repair. In fact, very, very expensive and very time-consuming to work on. Still, we were supplied with a courtesy vehicle until the Land Rover returned, fully functioning – not! The temperature gauge nigh-on exploded and Helen bit the bullet, drained the dwindling resources one more time and went out and bought the car she still drives today. It, at least, is ageing well, like my good self.

What with all the worries, and my injuries, to complete the set - so as to speak - the side panel fell off my trailer. So we didn't get out of the yard much until August in this stressful 2014. Consequently, having been confined to the yard for so long, we didn't achieve much - anything in fact - that summer.

Once we began to emerge from all these challenges and got out and about again, we just concentrated on training. This even included a session with Olympic eventer Matt Ryan, although that was rather disappointing because I don't think that he was used to a horse quite like me and he didn't hide his feelings. Helen also took me to a 2-day riding club camp, where I did the camping while Helen went home for the night. Camping is definitely not her thing. She did oblige us with her presence over the 2 days of training and I thoroughly enjoyed getting back into the swing of things after so much hassle.

This set me up for what was to be a busy Autumn. We were chosen to represent our riding club at the regional show jumping competition and (because of my celebrity status no doubt) we were also asked to be a guinea pig at a demonstration event for another riding club in the area. Helen's friend and our instructor, Marina, was instrumental in getting us this gig and I seized the opportunity to be an audience pleaser and entertainer that day. After all, I have a reputation to embellish. What was needed from me was an expert display of riding principles in front of a large audience. But loudspeakers and microphones aren't really my thing and I went down the comedian route instead, much to the joy of the spectators, I must say. As good as a rosette, I think!

In November, Helen took me back to the David Broome Centre, the very place where I had endured that life-threatening experience last year. As we pulled up and parked the newly panelled trailer in almost the identical spot, the unpleasant memories of those moments flooded into my mind. Once I was off the trainer all those woes vanished completely and we did our first dressage test in 14 months. I thought we did very well, considering, but we were nowhere near the top 10. However, our highlight of the year was coming 6th at the winter show jumping show at the same venue. I know that lots of people couldn't resist videoing the prizegiving at that event because my reputation for strange behaviour at presentations with loudspeakers in the arena had preceded way before me. Apparently, although I haven't seen the video myself, it appears as though I am dancing. Really? Anyway Helen, probably quite wisely, declined the opportunity to take part in the lap of honour with the other rosette winners. I didn't mind, I knew that I had already stolen the show.

We were both back on top!

CHAPTER 22

END OF AN ERA

As we moved into the last few months of 2014, things took another turn for the worse, and I really do mean worse. The highs and fun that we had so recently enjoyed disappeared into the ether. As if he had learned absolutely nothing, Steve at Blue House once again chanced his arm and attempted to bring me in from the field without the bridle or Chifney. Now, for sure, I, Kumakawa, was not going to miss this opportunity for fun (or you might call it misbehaviour). This did not go well. Unfortunately, when I reared up, I came down on Steve's shoulder and pushed him to the ground. Now, I am a large animal and I weigh over half a tonne, those statements should tell you my propensity for inflicting damage. The real damage, however, was the chain of events that this incident was to put in motion.

That evening, Steve telephoned Helen and relayed to her all the details of the episode. He told her that he would never bring me in from the field ever again because this was the last straw and, finally, he had had enough of my behaviour.

I knew it was all my fault but, when all was said and done, I was only being me and it was an accident. Sadly, it was poor Helen that really bore all the consequences. With Steve out of the picture, Helen was left with no choice but to go back to attending to my needs both morning and evening. This, alone, was incredibly difficult for her as we approached winter, but made increasingly so because of the responsibilities of her new job. She was in her very first term as a lecturer and had masses of teaching to prepare and deliver. The nights were closing in fast and, as I stood alone in the field, it was often very dark before Helen arrived to tuck me up. Sometimes I wondered if she was ever coming at all but I was well aware of how many things she had to juggle. I learned to be patient because, at least, I had the consolation of knowing that Helen had preserved her income and that I came very high up in her budgetary decisions.

I knew that Helen was going on holiday to Padstow for a few days in December and that she always visited relatives at Christmas. This year it was 4 or 5 days in Northumberland over the Christmas period. In normal times this would not cause a problem but, largely because of the difficulties with Steve, these were not normal times. There was no one at Blue House farm prepared to take on responsibility for me. Obviously, I wasn't as popular as I thought. With no help at hand, Helen was left with no option but to go to the expense of putting me in full livery for 3 weeks at Marina's yard. I know that the prospect of no mucking out for 3 weeks was soon offset by the weekly cost of the livery.

To illustrate how fate plays such a major part in all our lives, it was this period of 3 weeks away from Blue House Farm that gave Helen the space and thinking time to reflect on whether it was still suitable for me to return there. Her decision? I wouldn't be going back. It was like old times – changing yards after being claimed following a race, but I was a lot younger in those days. Wherever we were off to, I knew Helen would make sure it was great. I ended up staying with Marina until 1st February 2015 and then we moved to a lovely, friendly yard in Rudry, where we have remained until this day. Even Ross and Karen, my former owners, have visited me at this idyllic setting in South Wales.

Actually, 2014 ended on a happy note after so many downs and not many ups. However, before we move on to 2015, I have to tell you about the strange addiction that afflicted Helen for this and the next few years. It was an addiction that obviously satisfied her needs but was something I was not too happy, if not embarrassed, about putting up with.

If you're wondering what on earth I'm talking about, well, there was a craze at the time (and still is for many equestrians) for dressing your horse with matching saddle pads and bandages, completing the image by matching your clothing as well. It was me who had to suffer all the embarrassment as Helen spent loads of money on the accessories, even listing items on birthday and Christmas lists. I thought we looked a bit silly but Helen was well into it all. Our combined wardrobe took up a considerable amount of space and it was a bit of a relief, for me anyway when, a couple of years back, she was forced to sell most of the collection because she needed the money, probably to pay my vet's bills.

Oh well, if you must have an expensive man in your life, just take the rough with the smooth. Someone as special as me doesn't come along very often.

The addiction: "Matchy – Matchy".

CHAPTER 23

GRANGE FARM. HOME FROM HOME.

As I alluded to in the last chapter, my disagreements with Steve at Blue House Farm led to me having to slum it in full livery for the months of December and January. At this point, I feel I must point out that this unintended move happened, not through any fault of Nicola, the owner of Blue House Farm, but purely because of the unfortunate clash of personalities between me and Steve. Separation was the only feasible solution, regrettably. This superb luxury living took place at Drysgoed Farm under the wonderful care of my old friend and fan, Marina Evans. Drysgoed Farm was owned by a lovely lady named Polly Parker but we rarely saw her as Marina managed the yard.

Whilst I was staying in this 5-star luxury, Helen was faced with the problem of finding me a new, permanent home. Not an easy task, to say the least, when you own a horse that windsucks. Many yards have an outright ban on reprobates like me or insist that we wear one of the mediaeval cribbing collars. Legalised torture, I call it.

Helen had, a few summers ago, been to have look around a stable yard in Rudry, this was when I had my initial run-ins with Steve. It was a place called Grange Farm and was owned by a lady called Rae. She decided to give Rae a ring and inquired if she had a spare stable available to suit the likes of me. The news was good and a moving date of February 1st, 2015 was settled upon. It was still the middle of January, so I still had a couple of weeks to enjoy my spa break and get in some nice, gentle exercise.

Remember, I was currently spending my time at Drysgoed Farm and this idyllic spot was based in a small village called Efail Isaf. Helen loved taking me out hacking in this most beautiful of landscapes and my enjoyment of life was doubled because I was really able to take full advantage of the on-site training with Marina. Helen was living the life of luxury as well because she was exonerated from having to muck me out each day. I did miss her inspiring conversations, mind you.

It was during this month of pure joy and, probably, because of it, that Helen had her latest brainwave - dressage to music. If Charlotte Dujardin could do it on Valegro, for sure Helen McCarthy could do it on Kumakawa. The Retraining of Racehorses Association (RoR) held training days for all kinds of disciplines and, on this very rare occasion, they organised a *Dressage To Music* clinic at Pencoed College in South Wales, hosted by Amanda Birch.

Even though I am the first to admit that I am no dressage star, I was really chuffed that Helen decided to have a go at this. To my great satisfaction, after a first few minutes of being freaked out by the noise coming out of the speakers in the seating gallery, together with the inherent spookiness of the whole arena, I completely settled down and we both thoroughly enjoyed ourselves. Amanda absolutely loved me, of course, and I knew she felt that I would have Olympic potential had Helen been willing to give her the time with me. Sadly, we had other commitments. We haven't had any other opportunities to indulge our talents in this area since, but the whole performance can be found somewhere on video,

And so it came to pass that I arrived at Grange Farm on February 1st, 2015. It was a crisp, sunny day and the move went very well. Because of my windsucking addiction, I was stabled away from the main stable block on my own. The pros far outweighed the cons though. I have the most wonderful view imaginable and easy access to "my" fields. Plus, we have the empty stable next door for storage. It doesn't get much better than that. Another incredible advantage is how marvellously peaceful it all is, great for both me and for Helen.

To start with, I was turned out in a small, electric-fenced paddock. It wasn't very big at all and, being February, the grass was pretty sparse if not non-existent. The lovely Helen supplemented my needs with tasty hay. However, it took me very little time, indeed, to notice that there was far better grass elsewhere and it was no bother to someone of my ability to escape my confines to enjoy the fruits that my skill had earned. This earned me the first of many nicknames that Rae has christened me with – Kumadini, a Houdini clone whose escape techniques were known to him alone. Rae's other nicknames for me include, Fatboy – I have no idea why - and, most annoyingly of all, Kumi. Rae's nicknames are attached with the most enormous affection - but "Kumi"? Really?

Very relaxed in my new home

Helen's 18-mile round trip to Grange Farm is far from ideal, especially in the current circumstances when fuel costs are so high, and all the fantastic help that Rae gives us is so gratefully appreciated. Indeed, lots of people think that I belong to Rae and that's because she talks about me so affectionately. My greatest feature, so I'm told, being a loveable rogue.

Suffice it say, I settled in at Rae's from day one and, do you know what, although I am stabled on my own, I have never had a single issue with that. I guess the tranquil life suits me especially when I've got a live-wire like Daisy coming to check on me every five minutes.

.oOo.

For the uninitiated, "hacking" means "the riding of a horse for pleasure or exercise" and I suppose you can say that Helen and I did both of those at the same time.

The hacking around Rudry is exceptional. I am so lucky to be stabled there and those early months of exploration were super exciting. We used to go hacking with Rae on her ex point-to-pointer, Lockie (Lough Ennel), every weekend. It was simply, terrific fun. Lockie is still stabled at Grange Farm but he is now retired. Coincidently, he is also a chestnut with a white face, like me, and we look very cute together, if I do say so myself. Lockie had 13 point-to-point wins to his name and one win under rules. When he retired from racing, he did a lot of RoR show classes with Rae and was very successful. He clearly had a much better attitude for the game than I did, but I am not sure that he had as much fun? Rae has always owned Lockie, so including the time when he was point-to-pointing as well, that's why he is so very, very special to her.

I loved hacking around Rudry and found it a most fulfilling - nay exhilarating - experience, especially the many occasions I managed to eject Helen. She had never fallen off me before while we were hacking, that is until we explored the countryside around Rudry. The terrain and scenery were nothing like anything I'd ever seen before. So when, for example, I'd come round a corner and a duck flew across a pond, I would be in such a state of shock trying to take in what had just happened that I would spin around at the speed of light. Helen, unfortunately, had no option but to come a cropper and leave the sanctity of the saddle.

The best example of one these dismounting exploits performed by my mistress came when we were peacefully hacking down a small and quiet country lane, probably about lunchtime. Suddenly we came across a car, parked somewhat uncomfortably in a leafy hedgerow. This car, along with a large portion of the hedge, was bouncing up and down, quite rhythmically as it happens, with its two occupants clearly reaching a crescendo of ecstasy. To say I was shocked is the understatement of the year. I was a gelding, totally unaware of any behaviour relating to the loins but, even so, it was all a bit too much. I couldn't ignore what I was seeing, I just needed to get away! Because of the speed of my spin and sprint exit, I was completely unaware that, in fact, I left Helen behind as I made my excuses and galloped off home. Later, I overheard Helen telling Rae that I had deposited her right beside the offending vehicle and that she was nearly was exposed to an X-rated view of the proceedings. She added that the occupants of the vehicle, clearly experts and professionals in this kind of carnivorous performance, actually had curtains for the car windows and this, at least, prevented a few of everyone's blushes.

Yes, hacking is the best way to experience life and all its different facets.

Photo opportunity before hacking

CHAPTER 24

MARKING TIME

Since September of the last year when Helen began her lectureship at Cardiff University, her time had been almost completely consumed by work. There were always new lectures to prepare and the marking at weekends was both overwhelming and never-ending. All this made it impossible for her to take me anywhere on the trailer and, as my lifetime has involved a great deal of travelling from a very young age, this was something I missed quite a lot. So, in 2015, we couldn't function in our normal training mode until quite late spring.

That said, Rudry has a wonderful horse community and it wasn't long before Helen had joined us up with the Rudry Village Riding Club which had the advantage that most activities on offer could be hacked to, so they didn't take up all of the day. Through the club we started training with Judith Murphy who, prestigiously, is a Fellow of the British Horse Society (FBHS) and her personality and training style suited me down to the ground. We just seemed to click and I made my best progress in dressage through this lovely lady. You could say, "we would never excel but we tried hard." I love the training just as much as the competing.

Another major advantage of me living in Rudry was that we were only a 20-minute hack away from Sunnybank Equestrian Centre. I am not sure if I have mentioned this venue previously, but it was certainly to become far more frequented now that we were stabled so close.

By the end of May, Helen had fulfilled all of her teaching for that academic year and her final marking chores were under way. This gave her the opportunity to do something a bit more serious with me than just hacking. In fact, we did loads in May and June and we were quite successful too! We came home with ribbons from jumping and dressage at

Sunnybank as well as ribbons from jumping at Broome's at their summer show. I so lucky that we continued our training with Judith Murphy, and Marina Evans used to pop over to join me from time to time as well. Lucky and popular boy! Being in the riding club gave us opportunities to train with other instructors too. It was all magnificent fun and we were having a jolly good time. We even had another go at cross country.

July of this year saw me take some well-earned downtime after all those successes when Helen jetted off to Malaysia for her 40th birthday. She spent a few days in Kuala Lumpur before heading to Kota Kinabalu on the Island of Borneo. Quite the Jet Setter, our Helen. I don't think she is very good at birthdays and is always prone to leaving the country, when possible, to avoid any fuss. For myself, I love birthdays, just can't get enough of all those carrots and mints, extra strong of course. As said, this was Helen's 40th, a BIG ONE, and she deemed that it was worth the expense to put me into the very good care of my darling Rae for 15 days. I knew that, despite being away, I would never be far from Helen's thoughts and she from mine.

.oOo.

August saw us hit the ground running again and with the focused aim of competing in the RoR retrained racehorse challenge at the Wales and West Hunter Show. This was the show that we competed in during August 2013 and is one of the higher standard competitions that Helen took me to. All the work that I had done with Judith and Marina had boosted my confidence and mind was fully concentrated on achieving success.

The jumps weren't as big as the ones I remembered from before and I was a bit disappointed about that considering all the hard work and practice I'd put in at home over the bigger fences.

This gave me a complacent attitude in my jumping round because the fences were too small and, stupidly I had one fence down. As was my wont, I impressed the judges during our individual show (walk, trot and canter on our own) but, foolishly, got rather excited in the group phase once again. All that confidence, all that serious training, wasted.

To further my woes, this competition also required that the saddle is removed from the horse which is then led in by hand for the judges to examine its confirmation. I never score highly in this bit because I am, allegedly, "croup-high", sounds awful doesn't it! This is where the horses back end is higher than their withers and is characteristic of a young horse in their growing phase. Sad to say, I just didn't level off. Who could possibly believe that when I look so handsome?

As always, though, we took home some fancy ribbons and got a lovely set of photos with our amazing friend and groom, Alana, by our side, supporting us as always.

Because we had competed in the morning session of the show Helen, as always, keen to get her hands on some kind of rosette, had taken a chance and entered us for the RoR showing class in the afternoon. This is the class where I prance around the ring looking smart and do my best to behave. This isn't really my bag as I always find it too much fun to muck about in front of the stuffy judges. Last time - when the judge actually had to sit on me and steer me round the ring - things did not go too well. In fact, the whole experience was a dreadful disaster for both me and the judge. Fortunately though, this year there was no judge ride.

Thanks to Alana, I looked absolutely amazing and I knew it too. I was determined to seize my chance of glory and gave the display everything that I had. There is no doubt that I gave one of my best ever performances and my behaviour was exemplary in every way. Would you believe it, but I just wasn't this judge's cup of tea. My problem was I wasn't as flashy as some of the other horses. We left empty handed. I was gutted. As usual I eavesdropped as the judge explained my failings to Helen.

"Despite Kumakawa's improved behaviour, his stress is exhibited in his short, choppy stride. Show horses should be more exuberant with longer eye-catching strides."

I definitely had no idea what horse he had been watching? It certainly wasn't me.

It was a joy when Helen, as she loaded me on the trailer, whispered in my ear "At the end of the day, I'm still taking the best horse home". She made all the disappointment disappear.

My improvement (temporary, unfortunately) in the show ring saw us take home a massive haul of ribbons in the Sunnybank summer show later that month. We were even awarded the honour of being named

"Champions of our Section" and came home with a trophy – yet another one! This is how the scoring system works. If you are placed 1st or 2nd in any class, you go forward to a championship section where you compete against all the other horses that were placed 1st or 2nd in their class. I suppose the competition wasn't overly high, but we did end up Champion in one section and reserve champion in another.

Showing off

CHAPTER 25

NEED A REAR VIEW MIRROR

During this year I had to become accustomed to sharing the limelight with my companion Daisy. She was now 2 years old and Helen had been training her in agility for 9 months or so.

In September, 2015 Helen entered Daisy for her first real competition and she placed 3rd, winning a trophy. This was the prelude to a very busy few years when she competed both me and Daisy in virtually every competition possible.

Of course, when the Autumn term of Helen's second academic year at Cardiff began, her time with was again restricted by the demands of work. We did get time to do a fair bit of hacking and there were always lots of training activities at the Rudry Village Riding Club. The one thing that was almost a certainty was that I couldn't complete a year without creating a significant vet's bill.

To begin with, I had a bad bout of lymphangitis. Helen always blames this on my ill-disciplined behaviour but I maintain that I am just susceptible to this problem. You will remember from an earlier chapter that stern exercise is an excellent remedy for this condition and, consequently, on the Saturday we were out for a pretty strenuous hack.

Lamentably, up ahead there was a field occupied by a very ordinary horse. The only problem was that this horse was draped in a brightly coloured rug. This rug must have been brand new because the colours were so vibrant. I found this situation uncomfortable, to say the least, and I didn't see the necessity to go past such a hideous monstrosity. You know exactly how you feel when, for no obvious reason, you take an instant dislike to something.

Sadly, when you won't go forwards the only other way is backwards and, when you go backwards, it is always advisable to look behind you first. Now I have always had a very speedy reverse gear, as Helen would certainly testify to, having experienced it on many occasions and, confronted with this unacceptable blaze of colour, I engaged it straight away. Definitely should have looked behind me first as, suddenly, it was if I was having a thousand injections all at one time.

I had reversed into the mass of brambles that lined the narrow track that we hacking along. If I stayed still the pain was just about bearable but, of course that didn't solve the problem of "where do we go from here?" It was excruciatingly painful to go forwards as one of the "huge" bramble thorns had actually punctured my leg. It wasn't funny, so why did Helen have the giggles? I took a very deep breath and with one brave forward movement I extricated myself from this torture chamber.

The next day my leg was the size of an elephant's, not quite so amusing now. I thought that my pain threshold was very high, not so I'm sad to say. Helen could see that I was struggling big time and she had no choice but to call out the vet. On a Sunday of all days! More out of hours charges!

Once the vet arrived, he was extremely concerned about the amount of pain that, quite clearly, I was in. It was so bad that he thought that I might have fractured my leg or pelvis. To cut a long story short, I fortunately responded well to the pain killers and antibiotics and, guess what, he diagnosed a case of lymphangitis once I started to show improvement.

If I had broken my leg, no amount of drugs would improve the pain. I know that Helen thinks that I am a big baby when it comes to pain and she reckons that she can tell by the look in my eyes when something is really serious. Sometimes, she thinks I am just being a baby to grab even more of her attention. As if!

Having said all that, lymphangitis can be very serious and a horse at Blue House Farm had to be put to sleep because the problem wasn't caught and treated early enough.

So, a nasty vet's bill to end the year but, all in all, it had been a most satisfactory one.

CHAPTER 26

18ᵗʰ BIRTHDAY & BAD BEHAVIOUR

2016 was a year that threw even more challenges my way. This time it was my responsibility to be there for Helen. I knew that I was her ray of sunshine and that my mixture of mischief and fun was a recipe for a little bit of joy in her life. I love being her rock, she means the world to me.

Late in 2015 and through to early 2016 I knew that Helen was enduring some difficult personal and medically related problems. I didn't know exactly what was happening with her but I do know that she seemed to be on an emotional rollercoaster which was playing havoc with her both physically and mentally. I knew things were pretty serious when, from February onwards, I seemed to have retired completely. It was so unlike Helen never to ride me and it was all a bit confusing adjusting to this new lifestyle. I was aware that I was coming up to my 18ᵗʰ birthday, but I was a very young 18. My owners during my racing stardom, Ross and Karen, are "old people" in their 70s, but you'd never know it – it must have rubbed off on me because I'm the same.

I decided to play things by ear and see how things would develop. I knew for certain that it wouldn't just be workload keeping Helen from riding me, something more must have been involved. I discovered that Helen had needed to undertake a teaching qualification as part of her lectureship probation and, of course, that was very time consuming. I also found out from the grapevine that Helen was undergoing some special medical treatment and I hoped and prayed that all was going well. At least I knew in my own mind that my retirement was for a reason other than me.

Then joy upon joy, in March things took a massive upturn. Helen was back and I was unretired. Bits and pieces at first as we managed to enjoy the hacking again in the beautiful surroundings of Rudry village as well as joining in the training sessions at the riding club. Helen must have been better and I was over the moon.

Then such a special treat on my 18th birthday, March 13th. We went on a memorable ride in the glorious sunshine and Helen told me, only in the way that she can, how blessed she felt that she was still riding me at the age of 18. (Who'd believe that she would still be riding me today at the age of 24.) *Special* is nowhere near the word to describe me. I rather like *Legend*.

But I digress. On many occasions, due to the nature of the riding around Rudry and if we avoided the roads, Daisy was able to accompany us on our hacks. We had been unable to go as a trio until moving to Rae's and it was blissful. I adore it when she runs ahead of us and guides us as if she was the leader of the pack. You've heard of the "special one", well we are "the special two".

In the month of April, we won a dressage competition at Sunnybank and May saw us enter our first competition events at Rudry Village Riding Club. However, in true Legend Kumakawa style, I managed to embarrass myself at the first dressage event we attended at New House Farm. New House Farm is only a fifteen-minute ride from our own yard and it was also the venue for my training sessions with Judith Murphy, so I knew it well.

This dressage competition was being held in the riding arena, the actual space that Judith had used when she was putting me through my paces. Despite the dressage test being held in the actual arena, the warm up area and car park, for horseboxes, was in the field adjacent to the arena. Whenever I had visited New House Farm for my training, there had been nothing but a few ponies grazing happily and peacefully in this field. Imagine my disbelief and horror when I saw this field full of cars and horseboxes and people warming up the horses and ponies. Mind blowing!

I must say all this was starting to get to me. I did manage to keep a lid on it for both of our dressage tests but, once we had finished those and were walking through the field towards the exit, I sort of exploded and bolted, with Helen hanging on me for dear life, towards the gate. Now Helen has spent many years working with horses and has been privy to the industrial language of the horseracing world, which means that she is equipped with a vocabulary able to turn any air blue. This was an occasion to put this language to the test. Even I was shocked and I was going at breakneck speed at the time.

What the expletive releasing Helen was unaware of was the fact that, as we were careering headlong towards the gate, the Club Chairperson was close by with children in her presence. At that moment I think we came pretty close to being "asked to leave" the club. A very close shave but not terminal. Celebrity status has its benefits.

Everybody says that this kind of behaviour is typical of me. If I can't figure out what is going on and what I am meant to do, I panic and my fight or flight mode comes into play. This often has unforeseen consequences if Helen happens to be on board. It's just how I am I'm afraid.

Fast forward to just two weeks later at the same venue. We competed in a combined training event where I had to undertake a dressage test in the very same arena, followed by a round of show jumps in the very same field where I had displayed such tremendous speed and Helen had showcased her use of words.

This time, with no unpleasant distractions I knew what my job was, behaved impeccably and jumped brilliantly. It's all there in my locker when I want to get it out.

CHAPTER 27

SUMMER LOVING

The summer ensued with show jumping at Broome's and Sunnybank as well as training with Judith Murphy (dressage) and the occasional jumping lesson with the eventer Tom Rowland. Together with my friend Elano, we often headed off to Sunnybank to compete together as well as to attend sessions with Tom. On one occasion Helen and I were delighted to be offered a lift with Elano and his mum, Ellie. Helen always carries a camera, probably to make sure that I am accountable for any misdemeanours that I am responsible for, and that is why, to my utter shame, she has photographic evidence of me trying to rearrange the décor in Elano's trailer.

It is crystal clear now why it is that Helen always prefers to take me anywhere by herself and in our own trailer – she dares not risk the bill if I damage someone else's property.

One of the highlights of 2016 was meeting Simon Jobbins. Alana and Red had been having jumping lessons with Simon for several years at a lovely venue near Chepstow, Cledd Y Tan Farm. Alana had given birth to the beautiful Addison in the January of this year and it was taking her a little while to get back into the saddle. Throughout her pregnancy I had been unable to do many riding activities with Red and I missed those times. So, it was great news when she invited Helen and myself to join in her lessons with Simon. This was to be the start of something really special and we continued throughout the summers of 2017 and 2018.

Simon just had the knack. He wasn't soft, yet he wasn't a bully and he really got the best out of me and Helen. Although I love my jumping, I am the first to admit that I am not straightforward and this can be a problem for Helen as she is not the most confident of riders over fences and, sometimes that timidity transferred to me. There is no doubt that during our time with Simon, Helen's ability and handling skills improved out of all recognition and, considering she has been riding since 1988, she produced her best work in this period.

The improvement in our partnership over the next few years was incredible but, sadly, Helen could only make the sessions over the summer months, July through September, but we made the most of it - we loved those days so much. We would drive over, both us in a state of trepidation with butterflies fluttering in our stomachs. Simon would always have us doing something technical and high yet, several hours later on our drive home, we would be on cloud 9. The achievement, fun and satisfaction was immense and, of course, to share all this with Alana and Red was simply fantastic.

I also know how incredibly hard it was for Alana to be doing this only six months after giving birth especially as my friend Red tended to let her down most of the time. It's all about confidence really and, whereas I would sail over 99% of my jumps, Red continued to see monsters under each fence and, quite regularly, gave Alana a tough time by refusing to jump. Once he got going, he was fine, but it was always a very testing time for Alana. Red was the National Hunt horse and I was the flat specialist, yet it looked as if it should have been the other way round!

For whatever reason we didn't enter the RoR Challenge that summer but we did manage to show off our new jumping skills at Broome's that September and we were now able to enter the higher classes and jumped 90cm for the first time. I know I had the occasional pole down but, I'm sure I was a joy to ride. I'm not saying some things weren't difficult: for example, warming up with others was not my cup of tea at all. Too many horses and ponies send me crazy. I just like serenity and an uncluttered brain.

My naughty streak reared its ugly head again a week later when we entered the showing classes at Sunnybank again. Despite this being the venue where we had had so much success, I was not in the right frame of mind on this occasion. I felt like messing about and I did. We went home, under a cloud of failure, empty handed. I could see how frustrating this was for Helen. She kept telling me how stunning I looked and that, if I could get my act together mentally, who knows how far I could go. This line of reasoning gave me flashbacks to my racing career. I know that I had terrific talent but I wasn't prepared to show it all the time. I could have won loads more when I was racing but, clearly, some inherent character weakness prevented me from realising my full potential. I guess that I hadn't changed. It's who I am and we're all stuck with it I'm afraid.

As regards "show classes", I think that I am far happier with a jump in front of me, thank you. Prancing around a ring looking pretty doesn't appeal to me in the slightest.

All smiles with Helen, Alana and Red

.oOo.

One of the last highlights of 2016 was the Curre and Llangibby hunt fun ride in October. We did have a go at this once before but, now that I was able to take on the bigger jumps, it would be even more fun especially as we were being accompanied by Alana and Red. The ride is about 10 miles over the beautiful Chepstow countryside, so not something for the faint hearted, and there are optional jumps on some parts of the route. Quite often a professional photographer is lurking in the hedges, knowing full well that riders are suckers for a good photo. Who can blame them if they're riding a great looker like me?

It's a simple matter of plain fact that even a tiny fun ride has to be carefully planned when I am involved. The choreography around me has to meticulously organised because I am positively allergic to crowds. Quite often a ride will start at 10am with the riders setting off in small groups at 5-minute intervals. Lots of horses, lots of pandemonium, and very, very busy. Helen and Alana had worked out that, if we arrived as late as possible, we would likely be in the last group out, say about 1.30pm. Doing it this way meant that there was less chance of people overtaking us or crowding us which was a definite no, no for me.

We were a great team on those rides too, with Red being such a chicken when it came to jumping it was down to me to always take the lead and then Red would follow. This system worked brilliantly for Helen as well because she thought that I would be almost impossible to ride if I was behind another horse. I must say, I can't get my head around that reasoning at all as during my racing days I would nigh on always travel at the back of the field before unleashing my withering speed and whizz past them all in the last furlong.

Let her believe that if she wants. Even now, if we go hacking in company or are just walking down the road, Helen always makes sure that I am in front. Anything for an easy ride.

CHAPTER 28

TOUGH TIMES FOR HELEN

As we moved into 2017 there were non-stop whispers flying around the stables that Helen was having serious personal problems. This amazing person always put me first and never, ever wanted me to be worried about anything. However, it wasn't just the stories, Daisy and I both knew that not all was well. We kept our ears to the ground to find out what was happening and, of course, Daisy was in a far better position than I to find out the facts because she lived at home with Helen all the time. And, Daisy was extremely clever.

This female James Bond discovered that, for some time, Helen had been undergoing IVF treatment. I, certainly, was completely in the dark about all of this. When Daisy finally got to the bottom of things and found out that Helen, in these months, had endured 3 miscarriages, one particularly traumatic, I was shellshocked and numb with despair.

Daisy and I knew that, without the slightest question, we had to be there for Helen as she had been there for us on so many occasions. We would be her rock, both iron in our determination to be strong for her. With this IVF treatment, we also knew that that there could be more trauma and misery ahead. We were not wrong. Another miscarriage was to follow but our determination was buoyed by the fact that we both knew that Helen valued our company and support so very much.

We were Helen's saviours during this time and, more than likely, were the reasons why she didn't fall apart completely. It doesn't sound like much, but we were the reasons why Helen had to get out of bed each morning and, simply by being ourselves, we brought joy into her life at such a painful time. It was an honour to help.

Very rarely did Helen fail to visit me each and every day and, indeed, she continued to ride me when she was physically able to. Daisy was even luckier than me, as Helen was able to carry on training and competing her. I think that Helen really appreciated the distraction that we offered her in these harrowing times. Although she was only able to ride me sporadically during these months, we definitely made the most of it. I overheard her talking to Rae one morning and she said "Whenever you are planning to become pregnant, you never know when it will be the last time you will ride." As a gelding myself, I wasn't completely up to speed on matters of pregnancy but I sort of got the gist of what she was saying.

Luckily for Helen, I am not your usual run of the mill animal. Many horses, when they are ridden only intermittently or after a fair break, take some time to settle back down to the job in hand but, of course, we are talking Kumakawa here, nothing phases me. When Helen wanted to ride me, I was there for her, ready at any time and always as normal as I could be. Mischievous I may be, but very thoughtful.

.oOo.

On 13th March, 2017, I turned 19. Not a particularly interesting number apart from me starting to get really old, but Helen was determined to make it an occasion to remember and Rae certainly still talks about it today. I think that Rae already thought that Helen had a screw loose, but what she did for my birthday sealed the deal.

The winter routine for me is for Helen to visit me in the morning while Rae brings me to my stable in the afternoon where I would have a nice clean bed, a lovely full hay net and a tasty supper in my manger. On that day, Helen decided to make the occasion a little bit more interesting for Rae and me by providing me with a very special surprise. As the stable door opened, my expectation was that, perhaps, I might get a few extra luxuries on top of my not too bad daily allowance, considering that it was my birthday. But wow, wait a second, written on the floor of my stable was "Happy 19th Birthday" and not really written but spelt out in Bailey's high fibre nuggets, no less! My absolute favourite treat at the time. There's a lot of letters in that goodwill message, that was a huge amount of treats for me to scoff. Happy birthday, indeed, and a fabulous moment to remember forever.

The pair of us continued to join in with training sessions at the Rudry Village Riding Club. Dressage training continued with Judith Murphy and we enjoyed some absorbing and fun jumping lessons with a jolly chap called Ian Wright – no, not that one. I always enjoy the training part of my life, always have done right back to those racing days when I tore around Southwell racecourse, it's the fun part of the whole adventure and the Riding Club had such a great community feel back in those days.

Although the jumping wasn't as high or as technical as it was with Simon Jobbins, when I put my mind to it and was on top form, I really made some eyes pop out of heads with my ability. A flying machine, no less - when I put my best hoof forward.

There can be very little doubt that Daisy and I have a deep and mysterious connection, extra sensory you might call it. However, when this inexplicably broke down for a fleeting second, it looked very suspiciously like a deliberate and hostile act on my part brought on by a pique of jealousy. Not so, not so, not so.

What happened was this. Despite inconsistent training and competing, Daisy became a prolific winner on the agility circuit, often bagging several doubles on each outing. Outrageously, there were some unintelligent people who believed that I had become rather jealous of Daisy's ever-increasing rosette and trophy collection. What complete and utter tosh!

Consequently, when, by complete chance and totally by accident, I stepped on her, accusations that I did it deliberately to scupper her chances were flying around all over the place. My faith in people was thoroughly put to the test. How could anyone in their right mind possibly contemplate such a thing?

Everyone has seen the proximity in which we spend our time together and I suppose that it was kind of inevitable that something like this might happen. Generally, I have no problem with Daisy's herding instinct but, in this instance, the breakdown in communication led to my steel covered hoof, supporting approximately 550kg of top, top quality thoroughbred, making dangerous contact with her tiny paw.

Of course, I felt terribly guilty and completely devastated. I felt like bawling my eyes out. Daisy was my best mate, my carer, my guardian angel. For all the world I loved her. Yet I had harmed her and put her out of action for quite a few weeks, especially when the wound became infected and needed veterinary attention. I will never let anything like this happen again, but it is very hard when Daisy refuses to learn her lesson and insists on getting far too close to me. Good job that I have trained myself to be able to tip toe around the stable and the yard and make sure I follow all health and safety rules. Sadly, it can only be fingers crossed though. The day that I trod on Daisy was a one-off accident and not at all malicious, I pride myself on being a very gentle and loving soul.

CHAPTER 29

GINGER BOYS

Although severely burdened by so many woes, together with the strength that Daisy and I transmitted to her, Helen's own incredible competitive spirit gave her the inner drive to "carry on". Our outings were much more intermittent this year but we did manage to compete on a few occasions, not nearly as many times as in previous years but at least we managed some fun outings. In addition to Sunnybank, we would head over in the direction of Usk to compete in the Wye Valley riding club events. Alana was a member of the Wye Valley Riding Club so we were often encouraged to join her. Helen was blessed to have so many wonderful and supportive friends.

During June and July, she had a particularly tough and stressful time while, conversely, this led to me having things very easy indeed. Inactivity is not good for my weight and with my susceptibility to lymphangitis I needed to be careful with all things health related.

Very luckily, from my point of view, I knew that Helen didn't cope well with staying at home and relaxing, she's far too active for that lifestyle, and that is undoubtedly why we are so well matched and invariably in sync.

Consequently, I was as pleased as punch when, in August, Alana asked Helen to bring me over to hers so that we could join in with training sessions with Simon Jobbins. So it was that we headed over to Cledd Y Tan Farm every other Thursday until the end of September and enjoyed some of the most wonderful training sessions ever. I always loved being in Red's company, not only did we look like ginger twins but we were on exactly the same wavelength. I knew that I was a far more talented jumper than him, but so did he, so there was no animosity or faux competitiveness between us.

The girls said that we had both sprouted wings that summer and that they had never seen us jump so well. So much praise was coming our way that the two of them managed to persuade other owners to film our exploits and then the girls would dub the videos with music. How embarrassing for animals of our calibre.

That September Helen decided, as she would, to put all that training to good use by driving over to Howick, near Chepstow, for the Wye Valley show jumping competition. I really don't know what she was thinking about but she omitted the thoughts that would have reminded her that we rarely, if indeed ever, had jumped on grass. The thing about grass is that it often means other livestock may be present. Apart from Daisy and my horse mates, I don't do other animals.

I knew that Helen had realised her error of judgement the moment that the herd of cows in the field next door came into our path of vision. No wonder I gave the poor girl so much trouble during our first two classes in the competition, I know that I had seen cows before but how would I know if these ones were friendly or whether they would chase us off their property? Pretty hefty things, cows, you know. Fair play to me on this occasion, though, I put all that fear to the back of my mind and did it for Helen.

She called me "her flying Ginger" and on this day I managed to pull it out of the bag for her in the "Top Score" competition. We even collected a voucher as a prize that day but I didn't find it as funny as Helen when I overheard her tell a judge "This is one of the very rare occasions when Kuma related money had passed into my hands rather than out of them!" Quite amusing now all these years on, I suppose.

Anyway, nuts and bolts. The Top Score is a show jumping competition where each fence is allocated a set number of points. The higher or wider the fence, the more points you can accrue in the allotted time. There was even a "joker fence" which was much bigger than all the others and so worth a sackful of points. This was my day to be special for Helen. I knew that she was still going through still more of the multiple disappointments in her personal life and I needed to give her something really special to focus on. I jumped that huge fence twice - twice I say – once in each direction. What a sensational score, unbeatable.

You know, for all the banter about the voucher, it was the red rosette in her hand that really did the trick.

.oOo.

After getting over all that excitement, let's turn the clock back a few weeks to August 12th 2017. This date marked my 10th anniversary with Helen. A match made in heaven from the very instant we set eyes upon each other. No horse in the world could have been so lucky as to move from one set of adoring owners, Ross and Karen, to the bliss that I had enjoyed over those 10 years.

I knew that Helen would have something special up her sleeve to celebrate and I wasn't wrong. She had always fancied having a photo shoot - well she would, wouldn't she when she had a specimen of my calibre to model for her. Today was the perfect day for it because it happened to coincide with Ellie Thomas, a good friend of Helen from the local horsey community, starting up an equine photography business. The bonus for everyone in the circumspect atmosphere of the photo shoot was that Ellie had known me and my, shall we say, quirks for many years. Clearly, she was the perfect choice to capture some lasting memories.

Unfortunately, I am afraid that I had one of those days! I will say this though, with photography, it is a good idea to stick to the simple, tried and trusted poses, off the wall ideas are 100% likely to go wrong and big time.

Let me be frank when I describe this episode, the whole performance was born out of rank stupidity.

Influenced by the photos, on good old social media, of other horses in ridiculous positions, with riders doing crazy tricks, Helen decided to join the herd and show us both up.

Her idea? She was bent on achieving something rather idealistic and natural by having her photo taken on my bare back. That is a big no, no. It had never happened before and it certainly wasn't going to happen today! Painfully for Helen and super embarrassing for me, she chose her moment and jumped up on my bare back, thinking that it would be quite straightforward.

I had been the perfect horse for the whole time, calm, even a bit sleepy. I wasn't expecting what happened and the shock of a woman flying through the air to land on my back was just too much for me to handle.

Unusually for her, it never crossed Helen's mind that I most likely had never been ridden bareback before. That mistake nearly cost her life and would have left me as a quivering wreck forever. As she leapt from the picnic bench onto my back, (no hat either, another serious error) I had no alternative but to launch her towards the evening sun as soon as her bottom made contact with my skin. I didn't know what was happening, I was in a state of shock.

To make things much worse, the location that had been selected for this photo shoot couldn't have been more dangerous. Leaping on me whilst on the soft surface of the riding arena would have been far more sensible and appropriate, a gravel driveway, definitely not so. I vaguely remember regaining some cognition of what was going on and, even now, can see Helen flying through the air and landing on her back followed, milliseconds later, by her head striking the ground very hard indeed.

I knew that Helen would immediately realise how stupid she had been, I wasn't a placid riding school pony. I think that it was the extreme embarrassment that probably saved Helen, that day. Her head must have been spinning and thumping but she got up, dusted herself off and carried on as if nothing had happened.

I noticed, although I don't think anyone else did, that Helen had endured a very thick lip, a badly grazed arm and a blood splattered shirt. All in the name of a good photo. What are people like?

Helen, without doubt is a sucker for a good photo and the Curre and Llangibby Hunt fun ride doesn't usually disappoint. Once again Red and I flew around the Chepstow countryside in glorious autumn sunshine. I love autumn and I love that ride. I can't explain why but it truly is quality time spent with my best friends in the world, Red, Alana and the magical Helen. This year gave me an extra special feeling because it had been such a traumatic and testing year for Helen. Along with the incredible Daisy, we prayed that we had made some of this year bearable for our greatest friend.

Just to reassure you that I am most definitely the Kumakawa that, from previous chapters, you know and love, in November I suffered another bout of lymphangitis.

This meant another vet's bill but, more to the point, it was Helen's quick thinking and rapid actions that, once again, meant that I lived to feature in many more stories.

Yes, you still have years left to enjoy.

Me and Red with Helen and Alana

All smiles. Helen and Alana after a Simon Jobbins training session.
Incredibly proud to have jumped that high.

CHAPTER 30

I'M EXPENSIVE BUT SO WORTH IT

I knew from keeping my ears open and my nose to the ground that, at the commencement of 2018, Helen was having similar problems to those she had experienced during the last year. To make matters worse, her partner at this time continued to press very hard to start a family in spite of the fact that he had become unemployed. I knew that these difficulties were having a derogatory effect on Helen because she became rather distant in her engagement with myself and Daisy and we could feel just how unsettled she was.

The upshot of this problematic situation was that the relationship between Helen and her partner broke down completely and ended. Again, it was up to me and Daisy to do our best to put the pieces together and be the rock and the encouragement that Helen needed to get through it all. To cut a long story short, we are far better than any doctors, probably more expensive but worth every penny because our love and affection is priceless.

As usual my self-inflicted injuries were creating many vet's bills for Helen and she always insists that I love all the attention given to me by the farrier and the vet. She absolutely believes that I go out of my way to provide her with a big bill after causing her to spend an incredible amount of time organising all my treatment visits. I heard her tell Rae that all the latter can be more stressful than finding the money when you're trying to fit in a full-time job.

Worryingly, she also thinks that I am a bit of a Prima Donna when it comes to injury. She reckons that where most horses would be out of action for a week with a particular ailment, I would be out for a month. A hypochondriac, me? Well really!

All in all, therefore, the first half of 2018 was pretty quiet. However, when we did venture out, I really tried my best to put my best hoof forward so as to bring some joy back into our lives. I took matters into my own legs and added some impromptu dance moves into my dressage routine. This took Helen completely by surprise but put a big smile on her face when we came away with a rosette. We all know by now that Helen is a sucker for a good photograph but, would you believe it, whenever we went anywhere and won this year, there was no photographer.

.oOo.

Enjoying wonderful animals like me and Daisy actually brings humans together. Not only that, it gives us a chance to meet new friends ourselves. This was the case in the Spring of 2018 when an lovely lady named Connie arrived at the stable yard next door to ours. Because of Helen's unhappy situation at home - you'll remember how distant I said she seemed - Helen did not make any significant effort to connect with Connie over the first month or two that she was in the area.

However, as her demeanour softened, the connection became obvious and, once the pair of girls got their act together, it became a huge amount of fun.

Connie was the proud owner of Ted, a dark bay gelding and also an ex-racehorse who was 6 years younger than me, so 14 years old in 2018.

133

Bizarrely, Ted's racing name was "See More Bear", which if you look up the meaning of my full name, you might see a possible reason as to why we ended up as best mates. You see, Kumakawa is not only a famous ballet dancer, but a Japanese surname that literally means *Bear River*. What a coincidence! However, I would like to point out that both Ted and I liked to consider ourselves to be more akin to the ferocious wild type of bear, rather than the stuffed furry types that are intended for cuddling by little humans.

Ted and I became instant friends and we thoroughly enjoyed grazing in adjacent fields and hacking out together. I think anyone would call it a proper *bromance* these days. Clearly, we had a connection because, not only were both of us intelligent thoroughbreds, but also, we were both ex-racehorses (Ted actually won a lot more prize money than me on the racetrack, but I don't like to talk about that!)

Helen's and Connie's description of our connection differed in as much as they thought that we were both quirky, high maintenance and loved a visit from the vet and farrier. They actually believed that we were deliberately competing against each other for the number of injuries or lost shoes we could accrue in any one period.

We certainly did enjoy winding each other up when we were being ridden out and the two of us, together with Connie, provided the tonic that Helen desperately needed at that time.

Connie was the perfect medicine at the perfect time for Helen. Everything we animals did was vitally important for the health and mental well-being of our wonderful owner and friend, but Connie provided that extra tonic, such a special gift.

She was well motivated and hungry for success. So similar to Helen in so many ways, they both enjoyed plenty of training but liked the buzz of competing and coming home with a rosette or two.

I really thought that all my antics had finally drawn the curtains on Helen's showing days but Connie changed all that. There was I believing that all that nonsense was buried in the past but now we were going to be at it all again. Rightly, I feared the worst.

Connie, struggling hard to stay as my mate, managed to persuade Helen to compete in the RoR Challenge at the Wales and West Hunter Show again this year. The way that she achieved that incredible reversal of policy? This was the pitch. She desperately wanted to have a go at the Challenge with Ted and needed us there to provide guidance, moral support and charming company. What completely gullible soul would fall for that load of tosh? Helen, naturally!

So it was that Ted and I, with Connie and Helen in the saddle, spent hours hacking together through the countryside. It was during these rides that Connie would come up with all kinds of foolish ideas and, quite unbelievably, as if she was pacifying a younger sibling, Helen would go along with everything, simply everything. I'm sure, in her head, she had not the slightest belief that she would be going anywhere near the RoR Challenge again.

How wrong can you be! Come August Connie got her way and we all headed off to Chepstow to compete in the same class that I had lit up in so many different ways, so many times before. What possibly could go wrong?

That year the line-up was very competitive and some big names from the show world were there. Having Ted alongside me made the whole day enjoyable, and we had a blast. I came 3rd, in strong company, to Helen's utter delight, whilst Ted came in 7th at Connie's first ever attempt. Good boys, the both of us.

I was overjoyed that it was such a magic moment for Helen, and I knew how grateful she was to Connie for convincing her to go to that show again. I know that both girls had a fantastic time and all underlined by the fact that our faithful and lovely groom, Alana, was with us all to ensure that we all looked and behaved our best.

Dream team! Me, Helen and Alana

Showing off my RoR rosettes

CHAPTER 31

TOO MUCH, TOO SOON

Perhaps we were brimming with over confidence following our successes in the RoR Challenge, but certainly it didn't take much encouragement from Connie to persuade Helen to take us all on a trip to the Usk Show in September. We would be competing in the same class as before so no difficulties there. Helen and I had been through all this before and aiming for a prestigious final is a difficult prize to ignore. Bearing in mind that Helen was well aware of my distaste for those big country shows, where the sheer number of competitors and the huge crowds really get under my skin, perhaps she should have had the good sense to give this one a miss and simply allow herself to bask in the glory of our August achievements.

But Helen was having so much fun with Connie and Ted that the temptation was far too much for her in these delicate times. The omens were far from good.

On the day of the competition Ted left the yard with Connie earlier than us because he was entered into an additional class to me. Helen and I were going to meet up with them after that class because Ted and I were both going to be in the RoR Challenge.

However, when we arrived, we discovered Connie in an utterly flustered state. Ted had vehemently objected to the hustle and bustle of the show – I could have told the girls this would happen because Ted had such a similar temperament to me - and whilst competing in his first class, Ted'd over exuberant behaviour had caused him to lose a shoe and cut his back leg quite badly. Connie wasn't at all happy with both Ted's behaviour and the blood dripping from his leg injury, that she felt she had no alternative but to load Ted onto the trailer and beat a very hasty retreat back home.

So, Helen, Alana and I were left facing the music of the RoR Challenge alone.

It is very difficult to describe just how brave both Helen and I had to be after Ted's misfortune. Connie's absence was completely unnerving for the both of us. This had been her first attempt at taking Ted to a show like this and she had no idea he would be so upset by it. With all my experience of events such as these I could have prepared her for the worst but now it was me who was feeling completely unsettled and left trying to control my fiery side.

Helen managed to get me to our allocated ring and, although the warm up was a little too frantic for my liking, the number of competitors was smaller than usual and I knew quite a few of them. I thought I was well in with a chance amongst this lot and that gave me confidence and cleared my head. I was just in the mood for some jumping and destressing myself with vigorous exercise and jumped an absolutely superb clear round. I went on to impress the judges in all other aspects of the class until my nemesis event - when all the horses go round together. I simply cannot work it out. I canter, the others trot; I trot, the others walk. I blame the exciting atmosphere and the noise. I just go with the flow.

Thankfully, because I looked an absolute picture and jumped so amazingly well, the judges had no option but to rank me third and the consensus was that, if I hadn't been so much on my toes at the final element, I would have won by a country mile.

Nothing ventured, nothing gained. I did win the prize for the best veteran although, until these pages I have always kept my age under wraps. I look so young!

After such an inauspicious beginning to the day, we even qualified for the RoR Final at Aintree in 2019.

I knew that this was something that Helen wouldn't even contemplate, despite her genuine excitement at the time. But simply looking back at what happened at Usk this day and the unexploded powder kegs that could blow up without any warning whatsoever. A scenario emphasised by the forthcoming hardest part of this eventful day. Leaving the show ring and being taken back to the horse trailer/lorry park was like travelling through a war zone.

How I didn't trample on or inflict damage to any member of the public that day I will never know. Without any shadow of a doubt, I had reached boiling point by that time and I could feel that I was on the verge of exploding. Trying to pass other show rings and weave in and out of the public was almost impossible. Helen spent the whole time screaming at people to get out of the way but you simply would not believe that so many humans are blissfully ignorant of the damage that can be done by half a tonne of bouncing thoroughbred heading straight for them.

Helen was well aware that she had upset quite a few people that day, but better that than risking a serious injury to a member of the public.

After that reckless yet educational day, the girls decided, thankfully, that us boys did not need to experience shows like that again. We would stick to shows where there was a minimum of human activity and where only lovely temperament horses like me and Ted would be welcome.

.oOo.

Helen's fun times with Connie made sure that Ted and I had lots more hacking excursions and it was just as enjoyable listening to the girls as they planned our adventures. Connie decided that our next outing would be to the Ponderosa Equestrian Centre to tackle a British Show (BS) jumping competition.

All the show jumping competitions that Helen had taken me to, thus far, had been unaffiliated. I was amazed that she thought that we would be good enough for BS. One of the advantages of affiliated competitions is that the courses are designed by professionals and that they are held at prestigious venues. If you become a member, you can also win decent prize money. Very usefully, BS offers you the chance to jump "on a ticket" which that you pay a bit extra on the day to enter a BS competition without having to join fully.

Worth thinking about and worth putting our hat in the ring for, especially if we practised hard and with the right trainers.

That August and September Helen made sure that I continued to benefit from joining Alana again for her lessons with Simon Jobbins. I loved everything about those training sessions, hard, concentrated work but really good fun. Right up my street.

The blessing from these confidence building sessions was complete when Simon told Helen that we were, indeed, good enough to have a go at a BS competition and had been for some while.

Nothing to lose and everything to gain, Helen decided that we should give it a go. I really fancied the challenge and was well and truly up for the experience. I was a serene superstar all morning and behaved impeccably, surprising even myself. Into the show jumping ring we went, relaxed and ready to love every minute. I did to. I jumped amazingly well but it was a long old course and I rolled the poles of the last two fences. I was still exceedingly pleased with myself that day. I'm not one to play the age card but, even in 2018, I was a bit of an old boy!

Nevertheless, it was an item that Helen could cross of her bucket list and the whole experience did her a power of good. This was our first and last attempt at BS, we loved it and it felt even better because Ted and Connie enjoyed their day as well.

Furthermore, it was a joy that Alana was there to support us and such a shame that Red was so unpredictable that he couldn't be there to join us two boys.

So, after a summer of fun with Ted and Connie, they both moved on to pastures new in the Autumn. Connie needed to be closer to her work and family and couldn't stay in the area the winter. I was totally crestfallen and utterly heartbroken that I had lost a wonderful best buddy meaning that I would have to go back to riding solo again. Life can be really testing sometimes and devastatingly unpleasant. I was certain that Connie's enthusiasm and energy would be very much missed by Helen as well. Us three musketeers would definitely have to display that "one for all, all for one" mentality in order to keep ourselves going.

My final outing for the year was, once again, The Curre and Llangibby Hunt fun ride with Alana and Red. Another glorious Autumn Day with great company.

2018 was a milestone though and a sad milestone at that. I was getting older, Helen had so many responsibilities and concerns. We both didn't realise it at the time, but 2018 was the last time we competed, the last time we had a training session with Simon Jobbins, the last time we did a fun ride and so on and so on.

Action shot of me entering the ring for our first
British Show (BS) jumping competition

CHAPTER 32

HOW TO SOLVE ONE PROBLEM WITH ANOTHER

As the days of the December 2018 crawled by, it was evident to both Daisy and myself that all was not well with Helen. Instinctively we knew that this was a much deeper and more serious problem than all the upsets of the miscarriages caused by Helen's unsuccessful fertility treatment.

She was not herself at all and when she disappeared over Christmas and the New Year without so much as a word, we not only felt abandoned but we were desperately worried about our most wonderful mistress. Daisy and I were so incredibly lucky that we lived with such wonderful and caring friends. Clearly Rae and the others knew what had happened and what was going on, but it was left primarily to Daisy to find out the true facts. Daisy can get close to everybody and in any place.

It took time but she did her job, and we discovered the truth about Helen's situation. She had found out that her partner of 13 years, who had been so insistent on pursuing fertility treatment, had been unfaithful to her and was leading a double life with a woman who lived in Florida, USA. The numerous business trips he had been undertaking, alongside pursuing a family via IVF, had been fake. Understandably, the bottom had fallen out of her world, and she had fled to the USA herself to find solace and advice from close friends.

For us, January was a very unpleasant blur and we all knew that the trust in Helen's relationship had been shot to pieces and forgiveness could not be justified on the grounds of frozen embryos alone.

By the end of January, in this 2019, in spite of everything, Helen was doing her best to carry on as normal. In these circumstances it always amazes me how, somehow, I always come to the fore, although not always in the best of ways. Indeed, often it is my serious mishaps which help concentrate Helen's mind on other things than her own very serious problems. This was one of those nasty, if not dangerous times.

On a weekend in January, we had a training session with Judith Murphy. This was just the sort of distraction that Helen needed and the removal from reality was welcome to all of us. Helen had a smile on her face for the first time in ages and, as a reward for my part in this success, licking my lips, I waited for my obligatory tasty snack after riding. With horses, the reward gesture after exercise must only be a little taster, larger quantities of food are bad for us at this time.

Today's treat was a small handful of High Fibre Nuggets, remember them as my favourite on my 19th birthday? I gobbled them up like nobody's business but, hang on a second, I felt really rough indeed. When Helen offered me a second handful, I couldn't face them at all. Something dodgy was happening. I never refuse food. It crossed my mind – was I ill? I'm not really in pain.

Luckily for me, Helen is like a live wire. Alarm bells ring immediately if anything untoward occurs and I could see that she was taking in and processing all the tell-tale signs that I was, unintentionally, sending her.

I quickly went from my normal self to hanging my head very low. Neither Helen nor I knew precisely what was going on, I just knew that I wanted my head to be as low as possible. There were no other signs of discomfort at all, and this seemed to rule out colic as the problem. I remember pawing the floor a lot and not fancying either food or drink in the slightest. There was no other choice but for Helen to call the vet.

See what I mean? I'll always provide a major problem or something to distract her from her own disasters.

This was all occurring at lunchtime on a Saturday but, luckily, there was a vet not too far away. Par for the course with me, my symptoms completely flummoxed the vet and she confirmed, reassuringly, that I was not displaying any normal colic symptoms and that my gut sounds were as they should be. However, a worrying afternoon for all of us saw no improvement whatsoever and Helen just had to recall the vet. By the time she arrived in the evening it was cold and dark, and she could offer no other solution than to refer me to the veterinary hospital.

This was not a straightforward solution for Helen. She had no partner to help her, she was alone with me and Daisy. At that time, the vets that Helen was using had a referral hospital 45 miles away in Berkeley, Gloucestershire. A difficult journey via the M4 and the M5 which she was told to undertake immediately.

Feeling very unwell

What an absolute saint that woman is! It was so cold and so dark. I simply do not know where, burdened by so many awful tribulations, she summoned the strength from to complete this journey. She had the worry as to whether I would make it without collapsing on the way, so many difficulties. I knew that she must have been running on empty and was digging the deepest that she had ever had to dig, but she was doing it for me. To know that someone loves you that much brings huge amounts of responsibility. She had to get me to hospital to get me the help I desperately needed, I had to make sure that I survived to repay her love with my own after I had recovered.

We arrived at the hospital at about 8pm that evening, I think. Everything was all a bit of a blur. When I had got off the transport and was booked in, I remember that I had already perked up a little bit. I recall showing quite a bit of interest in all the expensive equipment that was scattered around everywhere. Once again, though, the vet had no idea what was causing my symptoms. All of my blood parameters were normal as were my gut sounds. The only thing of concern was my high heart rate.

To cut a long story short, short meaning a 3 day stay in hospital, the vet eventually diagnosed "choke". Choke in horses is not the life-threatening condition we associate with humans as the airway isn't involved. Typically for me, I wasn't exhibiting any of the usual signs for choke either, so this is why I had the vets scratching their heads so much.

It transpired that one of those High Fibre Nuggets had got stuck in my oesophagus when I gobbled my tasty treats and, to this very day, I have never ever been given the chance to taste those particular delicacies again.

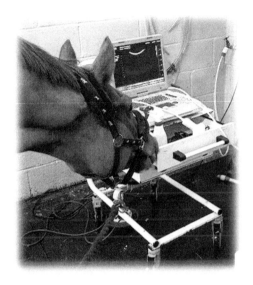

A bit too technical for me!

Back home and feeling better

CHAPTER 33

THE ONLY WAY IS UP

I'd certainly had my moment in the spotlight in January but, sadly I continued to be an additional source of stress to everybody at a time that they definitely didn't need it. I couldn't help it at all, but I was intermittently lame and despite visits to the vet no one could get to the bottom of the problem. I knew that this was not helping Helen at all but what could I do?

I could see the toll that the events of the year were taking on her and that her mental health was in decline. She couldn't ride me when she wanted to because of my intermittent lameness and when she did ride me, she didn't enjoy it because her negative thoughts were getting in the way. It was a perfect catch 22 situation with no apparent solution. The problem was exacerbated by the fact that the isolation of the stables seemed to put more pressure on Helen's mental wellbeing with the result that she was spending less and less time with me.

With her partner's departure, Helen found herself managing the household bills by herself as well as facing the costs of keeping me, especially with all the vets bills that I was generating. I felt so really guilty about everything. I couldn't help that I was getting old and I too felt my powers of reasoning declining with all the stress. Would I have to go? What about Daisy? So many concerns for all three of us.

Helen was trying everything she could think off to resolve all the problems and even advertised for a "sharer" to help with me although, with all my little (or big) foibles, I didn't think that there was much chance of success there. And I was right.

She thought that if she could have someone ride me for her, they could contribute towards my bills. This is quite common when horse owners find they have less time to ride or less money to afford their horse's upkeep. My intermittent lameness was a definite no no and I think my quirky reputation largely preceded me. No one ever came forward.

I completely understood that Helen's new financial situation would have far reaching consequences for all three of us. Luxuries such as competing and training me had to stop. I knew that she had to make a decision between competing me or Daisy. To compete both of us was an impossibility.

It's this one that hurts!

In a nutshell, Daisy was cheaper to train and compete, she was also younger and on an upward trajectory with her agility skills. I was 21 and my best days were definitely behind me. I just hoped and prayed that I wouldn't be discarded. Deep down I knew that Helen would never do that to me but I knew of so many horses who had been badly treated or just abandoned. These were desperately tough times.

For quite a few long, lonely months I felt extremely low and lost a lot of my self-esteem. Someone visited me daily and my basic needs were taken care of but I didn't feel special anymore. Reluctantly, I forced myself to accept that Helen's priority had to be keeping a roof over her own head, she had to put herself first for once and I was genuinely enormously grateful for everything she had done to care for me for all those years. I would do everything and anything I could to stand by her no matter what my situation. Love is a two-way street. I knew that, somewhere, I would always be in her loving thoughts.

Bad things always come to an end if you can just bear with them long enough and, towards the end of the year, life was stabilising somewhat.

Let's keep going, Daisy!

Helen was becoming acclimatised to her new financial situation and felt in a position to get me back out and about again. She did have the brilliant idea of selling up her vast "Matchy Matchy" collection to create some funds. And not before time in my view!

So late that November I was utterly thrilled to bits when she took me on a training session not too far away at Bassaleg. It was the first time that we had been out together in over a year and it really put a spring in both our steps.

I totally remember just how amazingly I jumped that day – jumping for pure joy I think – and it was clear to the both of us just how much we had missed our adventures together. That session was the spur that we both needed to put all the hurt behind us and move on. We were back, big time!

Little did we know that the Covid pandemic was just around the corner and that we would be confined to the yard once more.

Getting out and about again

CHAPTER 34

LOCKDOWN IS COMING

2020 started so well. Everyone was at the top of their game and we all felt buoyed from our outing at the end of last year. There was a joyful feeling in the air and we had lots to look forward to. Helen was in a positive and happy frame of mind, taking photographs of everyone and anything, a sure sign that she was feeling good and really getting back to her normal self. This will be evidenced by the very high photographic content which is heading your way.

As is the norm with us, something always happens to put a spoke in the wheel. Just pre-lockdown, in March 2020, I was happily strolling around the concrete and grass patch in front of my stable whilst Helen was getting on with the mucking out. She always blocks the doorway with a wheelbarrow to prevent me from getting in the way. I must say that this an everyday event and, when I see the wheelbarrow, I know what it is there for and just do a U-turn and walk away.

On this occasion, however, I must have had a mental block or something, one minute I was out enjoying the grazing and Helen was feverishly mucking out and the next I was marching into the stable. I honestly don't know what went on in my brain for those few seconds. I can't even remember noticing the wheelbarrow, those moments are a complete blank.

I suppose I got my legs caught between the handles of the wheelbarrow and became stuck. Also, in typical Kuma fashion, I panicked and went completely mental as I tried desperately to extricate myself from this infernal trap. Of course, with all this was going on, Helen was pinned in the corner of the stable while I was bouncing off the walls trying to escape the metal and plastic demons that were caught between my legs.

It didn't occur to me in the slightest that Helen was in serious danger at the back of the stable, in fact, to be frank, I hadn't even noticed that she was there, such was my panic-stricken mode. The incident got worse and worse and as I toppled onto the floor, a nasty, heavy fall onto concrete I must tell you, Helen saw her opportunity and rushed past me to make her escape. Now I could see the terror in her eyes and hear the anguish in her cries, not for herself but for me. This was an utterly horrendous event unfolding and I do believe that she thought that this was likely to be a fatal incident.

It goes to show how serenity can turn into disaster without warning, and in the blink of an eye.

Take a look at the photographs of the wheelbarrow after I had freed myself from it and, yes, I did walk away with just a few cuts and bruises. Yet another of my many lives taken up, made the Reading incident look like a picnic! I was quite sore for a while but, thanks to the much-needed skills of my physio, Karen Fuller, I was right as rain again pretty soon.

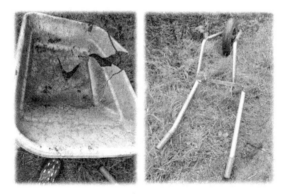

Kuma, The Destroyer

Now Covid took the reins and was calling the tune. Everyone was sent home from work as the UK wide lockdown was introduced on 23rd March 2020. Of course, we were then subjected to Welsh lockdowns and local lockdowns that included restrictions on travel and the formation of household bubbles. Luckily, visits to my good self were considered necessities and Helen travelled the 9 miles there and the 9 miles back every day to see to my needs although, in Wales, journeys were supposed to be restricted to 5 miles. That's the thing about bureaucracy, it always seems to be the opposite of common sense.

Fooling around before the seriousness of lockdown;
St Davids day 2020

.oOo.

The weather that spring was very kind to us but, whilst the gyms and parks shut and there was no workplace for anyone to attend, palpably, I could feel the draft of misery that permeated the air around all my human friends as the monotony of lockdown turned the screw.

Daisy and I were two of the very lucky ones because we had Helen in our lives. She was blessed too because she had animals in her life and we provided a therapy that not many people could call upon. Looking after us was an elixir better than any antidepressant and us 3 musketeers would stick together and pull ourselves through.

We revelled in the amazing weather and Helen took full advantage in the temporary reduction in her workload to enjoy hours of hacking with me and walking with Daisy. We are so lucky to have such beautiful horse-friendly countryside around the yard, Helen simply can ride me for hours on end. In recent times Helen had become accustomed to enjoying her own company and being in a bubble with her fur babies, as she calls us, and submerging herself in some serious gardening suited her just fine.

When most people were stuck at home, we had all these bonuses. We were extremely thankful to be so blessed.

However, I must say that Helen did seem to be a bit smug about being able to enjoy so much quality time with me when there wasn't much else to do although, occasionally, it all became a bit heavy, and I wished she would go back to work and things would go back to normal. Only occasionally, I'm just saying.

With Covid and all its restrictions continuing, there were no riding club activities or any competitions to aim for, so it was very much a bit of the same throughout the year. Along with hacking, we sometimes took ourselves into the arena to lunge or do a bit of dressage training, anything to keep the brain cells ticking. Plus, of course, it is very important to keep an old boy like me supple and those activities were an important part of our regime and still are today. As well as circles and transitions we do a lot of stretching, all very important for strength and flexibility.

Being super intelligent and super public-spirited Helen decided to put a ban on jumping and any other high-risk activities to avoid putting more pressure on the NHS, so she made sure that I kept all four feet on the ground and that all wheelbarrows were safely tethered.

The three musketeers

CHAPTER 35

OLD FRIENDS RETURN. IT'S CHEER UP TIME

Whilst the monotony of Covid continued into the Autumn, our hacking was made even more enjoyable as Connie and Ted returned. Us boys were reunited, and it seemed as though Ted had never been away. The bromance continued as Helen's single head hacking photographs returned to being double heads. Sweet! It is really amazing just how good horse's memories are, Ted and I remembered each other as if all our escapades were just yesterday - and it was wonderful to see Helen brimming over with joy at the return of Connie. They both were over the moon to be able to spend so much quality time with their boys.

One of my fondest memories of that Autumn was the fact that the Rudry village community decided to cheer up all the residents by holding a scarecrow competition in the run up to Halloween. The theme of the scarecrows had a serious side as well because the idea was to encourage drivers to slow down as they went through the village. Fabulously, they kept popping up everywhere and the two girls enjoyed hours of amusement finding them on our rides and then posing with them to take photographs.

Ted and I were usually startled by such dangerous beings as scarecrows and the slightest touch by one of them would normally instil terror into our loins. Now they were cool and we loved investigating them, being intrigued rather than scared. Both Ted and I have spontaneously inquisitive natures and I am sure that the girls found our engagement with the scarecrows highly amusing.

The autumn rides without thinking about training or competing were a welcome break for everyone and a vital mental relaxation for our stressed-out owners. I knew that Helen found on-line lecturing soul-destroying and that she struggled teaching face-to-face these days because she had to be so heavily armoured with Personal Protective Equipment (PPE). However, somehow, the symbiotic relationship between myself and Ted seemed to transmit vibes of serenity and joy between the two women.

As we rolled on towards Christmas, not a lot had changed for the three of us although the three became four when Helen introduced us to her wonderful new partner, Rhys. It was so fantastic that he thought the world of, not only Helen of course, but also of me and Daisy. What a fabulous Christmas present! Helen got a second brilliant gift when she was promoted to senior lecturer at Cardiff University, at least that will help with future vet bills, so no worries on that front!

This will be chapter inundated with photographs, I'm afraid, what with the Christmas photo shoot that Ted and I had to endure. Be ready to sit back and take them all in.

Here's the (paper) chain of events: the girls dressed us up in tinsel, copious amounts of it, in fact, and on Christmas day itself, the four of us went out for a 2-hour pre-lunch ride. However, they nearly missed their respective lunches due to a fallen tree in the woods which caused them to worry that we might have to re-trace our steps, adding another hour or two onto our journey time. Ted and I were both looking forward to our Christmas lunches and presents as well, so we carefully negotiated this fallen tree by stepping over it with supreme bravery, no wheelbarrow syndrome here, even though, if truth be told, we were both a little panicky.

All in all, despite the country being in the middle of a pandemic, I think I had a really lovely 2020. I was under no pressure to perform, I enjoyed the miles and miles of riding and, above all, the return of my wonderful, best mate Ted.

CHAPTER 36

SOMETHING IS NOT QUITE RIGHT

2021 was to be a strange and frustrating year. Covid was very much still with us and, in Wales, life was far from normal. Still, Helen and Connie made the most of things and carried on hacking with me and Ted, using all available film as they catalogued our adventures. I remember with great affection a very special 2-hour ride on Easter Sunday, when there wasn't a cloud in the sky.

Optimism in the yard that some sort of normality might return soon was an air that breezed across all of us in the stables as well. We were all champing at the bit for some long-term action as all the owners leapt at any chance of any training opportunities. Ted and I were over the moon when the girls took the plunge and decided to do a bit of jumping. Obviously, it had been quite a while since either of us had done any such thing and, as this is a pretty demanding exercise, the girls, sensibly, eased us into the action and took their time in getting us both "jumping fit".

As always, I was as keen as mustard and I must say that Ted showed a lot of promise too, considering the lengthy break we had been forced to take. The girls had built some impressive jumps in the arena at Grange Farm and our enjoyment increased as we really got stuck into the exercise.

Of course, I was full of enthusiasm. As a natural born jumper, I was brimming with enthusiasm and joy but something wasn't quite right. I would still clear my fences with great dexterity but, on landing, occasionally everything felt wrong. The only way I can describe it is that I felt a little bit unbalanced for a few strides after landing from my jumps and this only happened when Helen was riding me on the right rein (clockwise to any non-horsey folks).

Helen was well aware that something wasn't quite right but she put it down to the long lay-off that we had from jumping and we just cracked on. I am absolutely certain that Helen's reasoning was that, because I am so sensitive, a baby in other words, if something was very wrong then I would stop jumping altogether and I wasn't displaying any of those tell-tale signs. To be honest, it had been such a long time since I had enjoyed so much fun that I didn't really notice any discomfort at all and the desire to continue all that pleasure seemed to block out any other feelings.

As well as the girls jumping us at home, Ted and I were reliving our foal-hoods by jumping any fallen logs we encountered on our rides through the woods. The girls were determined to get us boys match-fit again (do their ambitions for us ever abate?) and this creative freedom was their fun way of supplementing what we were doing at home.

Also at home, Helen continued to insist that we did a fair bit of dressage training because this is so good for keeping old guys like me supple as well as fit and she supplemented this with lots of lunging, which is also excellent for fitness and suppleness. Coincidentally, lunging was also Daisy's favourite form of exercise. She really puts everything she's got into her lunging and is so determined to be "top dog" that she has worn a path around the manage due to her running back and forth whilst lunging. Daisy is some fit animal and so supple that she's almost fluid. I love her!

We enjoyed our jumping at home that Spring and riding club activities had slowly started to emerge again. Then, out of the blue, Helen and Connie were offered the chance to have a show jumping session with a young, Brazilian showjumper named Bruno Freire. What made this fantastic opportunity even more exciting was that the session was being held at Ruperra Castle which was built in 1626 by Sir Thomas Morgan at Machen in the borough of Caerphilly. Now a Scheduled Ancient Monument, the castle has a long and interesting history but the stables area has been renovated which makes it a perfect and special place for Bruno to often set up base. Ted and I knew that we had better brush up well because the girls certainly would not be missing this photo opportunity.

That Saturday afternoon in late April, in glorious weather, the four of us set off on our 45-minute hack to get to the castle. Initially, the building was hidden from view by the foliage which decorated both sides of the stony and bumpy track which meandered down to the castle. None of us, horses or humans, had ever been close to the castle before and we were all completely gobsmacked when we first set eyes upon it.

Stunning! A single word that totally expresses all that our eyes were taking in. An honour to be performing in such a hallowed space. I was inspired and I knew that I would put on a great display.

Riding amongst the bluebells, Spring 2021

I had the most wonderful time, ever, and Helen had her hands full trying to control my enthusiasm. Although it was far from jumping the heights that I had managed pre-Covid with Simon Jobbins, I felt hugely accomplished and Bruno was full of praise for me. Honestly, he could not get his head around the information that I was, at 23, a year older than him. Life is full of strange and amazing facts; this one was right up there!

On the downside, Ted and Connie did not enjoy such a good day. Like Red, Ted can become quite problematic to ride when jumping comes onto the scene. The two of them have a lot in common; they either put the brakes on and refuse to jump, or simply just don't pick up their feet and knock all the poles down. I have tried to help and encourage them but, unfortunately, they just do not possess my bravery and skill.

Ruperra Castle

Sadly, on that day, Ted was very difficult and Connie was quite frustrated about everything. Consequently, Helen and I had to keep our elation under wraps but, underneath, we were bubbling with excitement and joy. The whole aura of that day made me feel so good that I sprouted wings, and it was such a magnificent feeling after not having had the chance to do any proper jumping for so long due to the pandemic.

The highlight? One of our "King of the Castle" photographs was subsequently selected to feature on the front cover of the Riding Club Yearbook!

CHAPTER 37

IT'S NOT ALL HIGHS

A few more jumping sessions and a dressage session following on from our adventures at the castle proved to be concerning. I just didn't feel right and, whereas the euphoria of getting back into the swing of jumping had masked those problems that Helen had noticed earlier in the year, this time both she and I were worried that I was well below par and becoming intermittently lame more frequently.

Helen took the decision that she could no longer ignore what was happening to me and so she abandoned all her plans for the summer and decided to seek veterinary help. This also created somewhat of a problem for her because, by all accounts, she had lost faith in the inexperienced vets at her current practice, a difficulty exacerbated by its loss of most of the more knowledgeable practitioners.

To cut a long story short, no long term or sustainable remedies could be found so it was hacking for me for the remainder of 2021 while ingesting anti-inflammatory medication every other day. No-one, including me, was able to determine whether it was my left front leg or my right hind leg that was causing my problems. All the vets were reluctant to fully investigate what was going on because of my age and, indeed, Helen and I found it most frustrating that they simply put everything down to my years.

We horses have the same problems as humans, when you get old the majority of people just want to forget about you. Out of sight, out of mind.

Not in my case, I've got Helen.

While I was below par, Ted followed suit. He also was having health issues and one of those included a flare up of his gastric ulcers that summer. It was hardly surprising that the girls were becoming rather frustrated, there were no riding pleasures to be enjoyed, not even a half a mile hack.

With Covid restrictions easing, I absolutely knew that Helen would not be able to sit on her hands and do nothing. She would definitely find something out there for me to participate in, even if she had to fit me with wheels.

So it was that her exasperation got the better of her and she decided to take me to a local show at Sunnybank Equestrian Centre. As I wasn't in full riding work, Helen thought that it would be perfectly acceptable to enter me in two of the in-hand classes, especially as I looked in wonderful condition despite doing next to no work at all.

I was entered in the "Best Veteran" and "Best Ex-Racehorse" competitions. Usually, a complete doddle for me!

For Helen, this turned out to be a day of enormous regret. Why did she do it? It was like entering the gates of Hell.

I hadn't competed since 2018 but she thought that a local show would be just fine and stimulate my brain. She couldn't have been more wrong.

Whether it was my aches and pains giving me gyp or I just didn't fancy being dislodged from my home comforts, today, this was not at all up my street. As the experience seemed to close in on me, I found myself getting more and more stressed out and, although I knew what was happening, I just couldn't stop myself from behaving more and more badly.

Even though we were at an indoor venue, Sunnybank can be quite busy with a burger bar and many rows of seating in the viewing gallery, with people faffing about during the classes. I have experienced all this so many times in the past, I just can't explain why I found it all so upsetting that day but upsetting and annoying it was.

Helen could barely keep hold of me during the classes. I heard her say to one of the other competitors that it was worse than leading a 2-year-old around a racecourse paddock for its first race. I can look back and think it's funny, but Helen didn't think so as I was pulling double and plunging forward, spinning her around and spinning around her. She definitely wished that she had stayed at home that day and took no pleasure whatsoever from the entire performance.

I guess that it was bad enough not being able to ride me because of my physical condition but being asked to leave an in-hand veteran class must have been totally demoralising. "Never again!" she fumed. "Being kicked out of a class at the age of 23 is nothing to be proud of!" Looking back now, I think it was hilarious!

.oOo.

With both us boys totally out of form and me, especially, on the naughty step, we were in complete trepidation about what these crazy women would think up next. Whatever they came up with, we would just have to get on with it, otherwise we would be out on the street. Odds on it would involve a camera but who would look silly, us or them?

It was them!

They decided to have yet another photoshoot but this time with them as the stars and us as the extras. They made the decision to wear dresses and make it a formal shoot, the pictures being taken throughout "golden hour", the period of daytime shortly before sunset during which daylight is redder and softer than when the sun is higher in the sky. Connie was friends with a young and very talented photographer named Abbie Kyte who had been photographing dogs and was keen to add horses to her repertoire. The girls pretended that this was her job at hand but really, they just wanted some great pictures of themselves to cheer each other up.

Honestly, if anyone had witnessed the build-up to this event, they would have thought that one of either Connie or Helen was getting married and the other was going to be the chief bridesmaid.

Daisy let us boys know, finding dresses for this occasion had been a very serious business indeed and now shoes or boots, hair and make-up all became world shattering issues. Even the long-term weather forecast had been meticulously studied to ensure that the event was booked to take place on the evening when the sun would shine beautifully and guarantee those perfect golden hour shots.

To compliment matters, Ted and I were scrubbed to within an inch of our lives! It would have been a lot easier if we had performed well in our competitions; a lesson well learned.

Notwithstanding, the photoshoot was a huge success and boosted everyone's mood enormously. Abbie took some great pictures of us with the girls as well as us on our own but, I have to admit, that our wonderful owners did look pretty special this night and the images that Abbie captured did them full justice.

Not long after enduring all that heavy duty grooming and preening, here it was happening again. What was going on now? Surely this monster clean up wasn't going to become the norm?

It was the evening of 1st September 2021 and Helen was scrubbing and polishing me like mad and as if I was going to be the star ride at a real wedding. As she worked feverishly on my appearance, I heard her tell Rae that my former owners, Ross and Karen were coming up from Hertfordshire to visit me.

It would be like old times at the racing stables. I loved it when those two came to the stables for our weekly love-ins and, besides, Karen always brought along copious amounts of Extra Strong Mints. Ross was getting a bit old now, like me, but he had written his autobiography when he was furloughed during lockdown and was now in a position to offer some advice to Helen's new partner Rhys, who was working on his own book.

We had a fabulous reunion that morning before the four humans abandoned me as they all went off for lunch, taking Daisy with them, of course, to the dog-friendly pub. It was horse friendly as well but I'm just too big to get inside, better off at home. Still, it was a very special day for all concerned.

CHAPTER 38

A SAD GOODBYE – FOR THE SECOND TIME

The remainder or 2021 was very uneventful. Helen and I continued mostly hacking, with some light dressage training thrown into the mix but, annoyingly, I was permanently on anti-inflammatory medication. I knew that Helen found this extremely frustrating as I was fully capable of being ridden. She did manage to get me to a few training sessions at the end of the year but I knew that, at the back of her mind, she was concerned that she hadn't discovered what was wrong with me and worried that she was just masking my health issues with the medication.

I was clear in my own mind that I had far too much energy and sharpness of brain power to contemplate retirement, so we both had to accept that things would have to go on as they were.

All in all, with everything that was going on in the world, 2021 had not been that bad a year but it was about to come to a sad end for the both of us.

We had enjoyed every second of our second time with Connie and Ted but things change. Connie's glamourous and exciting new job meant she had to move away yet again. It was a bittersweet moment for me and Helen, we were so pleased for Ted and Connie in their new venture but upset that they had deserted us once again.

Actually, I didn't yearn for Ted like I did the first time he left and the fact that his stable was soon filled by an 11-year-old grey mare called Penny might well have had something to do with that. Even an old boy like me can be well and truly perked up when a much younger bit of skirt might show an interest. For sure, I think that Helen felt this departure much more keenly than me. Christmas can be a difficult and very demanding time of year.

However, there had been some great pluses for Helen in 2021. She had been appointed as a trustee of the National Horseracing College and become an auntie to George, who was born 10 weeks premature. The McCarthy family also gained a new 1-year-old dog, Belle, adopted from a rescue centre after a rough start to her life.

Also, agility competitions had restarted after an 18-month break due to Covid and Daisy had brought home a few red ribbons. It was lovely that Helen was able to start training Belle for her agility career and what that all the nicer was that it gave her something to focus on while I was on the bench, so as to speak.

Looking smug with my new friend, Penny

Daisy & Belle together

My first meeting with Belle

.oOo.

To be blatantly honest, neither Helen nor myself could find much motivation to do anything at all as, quite unbelievably, 2022 appeared on the scene. I found it so hard to digest the fact that this would be my 15th year in the care of my own wonderful angel, Helen. I think the old adage, "Trouble and Strife" really needed a sex reversal in our case.

I knew that the massive loss of Connie weighed heavily on Helen's shoulders but it was her concern for me that really affected her inclination to move forward with anything remotely strenuous. Because I was constantly being dosed up with anti-inflammatories, I realised that Helen knew that I had some kind of problem but could not work out what it was that made me so unsound.

I was well aware that Helen completely had lost faith in the vets that had previously treated me and was at her wits end. Then in February something in the inner workings of her brain snapped and she made the decision to move away from all known practitioners and try someone, although not totally new, who had been well out of the "Kuma-loop" for several years. The hope was that this vet, with a fresh pair of eyes and an uncluttered mind, would be able to come up with some sort of diagnosis for us to move forward from.

The complication was that I was so very well in myself, full of beans in fact. I was rideable in the gentle hacking sense but something was wrong either with my right hind leg, my left foreleg or both. I couldn't work it out myself, what chance would a vet have?

So it was that Helen took me to see David Agnew MRCVS, who runs his own practice near Caerphilly, very handy because it was so close to our yard. My memory, red hot as usual, meant that I recognised David immediately and recalled him treating me many times before, but in the dim and distant past. The day that Helen chose to take me to see David was horrendous. The wind was strong, and the rain was horizontal. Luckily it only took us half an hour to get there and I was super impressed with the whole set up. The best thing about everything that happened on that day was that the vet had an indoor arena where I could be examined in the dry and where we both appreciated the clemency it offered from the elements.

This fellow was very demanding indeed and had me walking, trotting and cantering until the cows came home. Then it was the X-rays. My front feet seemed to be the area of most concern and I wondered if the X-rays would reveal any secrets.

Sure enough, at long last, some defining evidence to prove what the problem was. The amazing thing was, I was the one with the problem but I could not, for the life of me, work out where that problem was.

The diagnosis: something called medial-lateral imbalance of the left pedal bone. Very self-explanatory! In simple terms, the bone in my foot was 5mm lower on the inside than on the outside. Eureka! This could be a source of pain as the bone on the inside is getting bruised all the time because it is so much closer to the ground. See for yourself!

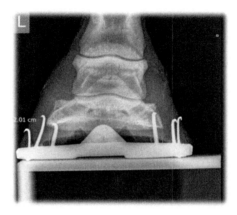

David's treatment plan was to send my X-rays to Sam Rooney, my super farrier, the fourth emergency service hero from a much earlier chapter, so that he could design and fit me with some special bar shoes. Regular horse shoes are U-shaped but bar shoes have a piece of metal that connects the two heel points. What a great and simple solution; disperse all those hundreds of kilos of weight in a much more Kuma- friendly way.

It was like I was reborn! I was both flabbergasted and delighted with the new regime, I was no longer lame. No more anti-inflammatory drugs for me, I felt like a teenager again. I got re X-rayed again in April and David was so pleased with my progress that he advised Helen to put me back on a normal exercise programme with the proviso that I should wear bar shoes on both front feet for now. You just can't beat comfortable shoes.

I didn't feel too bad for Helen either, when I found out that the regular 6-week fee for my shoes had only gone up from £80 to £100. A small price to pay for my comfort and her peace of mind – there was the saving on anti-inflammatories to be taken into account as well, of course.

Spring turned into summer in this, the final few months of my story so far, and I was, and am, a much more comfortable and happier Kumakawa. I'll be absolutely honest; I am not 100% right but I am 24 years old for goodness sake. Things get a bit creaky at my age but I just get on with it and enjoy life as it comes.

David had another good look at me in June, with more X-rays on my feet and back legs too, this time. For sure, he found some arthritic changes in both back legs and prescribed some steroid medication to help, but I can't and don't expect Helen to keep running me over to see him every five minutes. Funnily enough, that would be pretty tricky right now as Helen doesn't have the Land Rover available for transport anymore: its engine seized in July.

I heard her tell Rae that she needed to marry a millionaire, and pretty damn quick. But then, I could always write an incredibly successful autobiography. That would definitely help!

Despite all my ongoing minor issues this summer, I have been feeling really well recently and I know I look good. Helen can read me like a book and, when she sees the pages unfold so well, I know the lure of competition will be hard for her to resist. RVRC had their 10-year anniversary summer show planned for a weekend in August and, in spite of my seriously unruly behaviour at Sunnybank last year, behaviour which Helen swore marked the end of my showing career, I knew that she was continually being cajoled into taking me along and would find it very hard to say no.

I think she breathed a huge sigh of relief when the event had to be cancelled because of the heat wave.

Notwithstanding, the show was rescheduled for the first weekend in September, but its location was moved to Sunnybank Equestrian Centre. We had history! Recent history! Thrown out last year for misbehaviour. Surely, she wouldn't be tempted?

Everybody and their brother were putting pressure on Helen to take me along. They needed a celebrity and it was me. The venue was so close that lack of a Land Rover was not an issue but would she succumb?

Of course, she would!

Her competitive spirit got the better of her, after all she knew how well I was in myself. She put her thinking cap on and worked out a plan which might change the dynamics from last year's fiasco.

Way back when, Karen Fuller, the physio, had suggested to Helen that she should try me in ear plugs. These, she thought, would help keep me calm because I can be so reactive to noise. Helen, in the last chance saloon as it were, bought some and it was all systems go. And they worked!

I was far from perfect but the ear plugs helped me cope much better with the noise of the crowd clapping, the burger bar and spectators moving to and from their seats. First, Helen entered me in the in-hand veteran class. Ear plugs or not, I always seem to feel the need to relieve my stress levels in some way or another and, today, I thought that the reins were extremely tasty. Considering that I did spin around Helen the first time the crowd clapped, I coped very well after that, and we were rewarded with a very creditable 2nd place.

Onwards and upwards as they say. Always looking for more, the unsatisfiable Helen, now full of confidence that her earmuffed mate was on a vertical trajectory, decided that the "ridden veteran class" would be right up our street. Bang on! Hallelujah, we won it! However, it was still a very nerve-wracking experience for Helen when 10 of us cantered around the ring together. I could feel myself getting stronger and stronger, the urge to race was real and present, but I held it together magnificently and obviously impressed the judge.

By late afternoon, horses that had come 1st or 2nd in any ridden class that day were eligible to enter the championship class, which was the last class of the day. I couldn't help but put my best hoof forward yet again and we were awarded the status of Reserve Champion. Ear plugs turned out to be my secret weapon and who knows what heights we would have scaled had we tried them earlier.

I am so happy to end my story on such a high note and who knows what Helen will have planned for the future? Will she enlist me in The Veteran Horse Society and enter me in their show classes at the age of 25? Never say never.

I am so grateful to all the wonderful people that I have talked about in this, my life story. You have all been an absolute joy to know and love. My life has been very special, and I have lived and loved every minute of it.

Still got it!

LEGEND

Part of the proceeds from these books will go towards
supporting Kumakawa in his retirement.

Visit www.Kumakawa.co.uk
For further information including
Videos and photos of Kuma and Daisy
Information about Kuma's children's book:
'The Adventures of Kumakawa – The Horse That Will Try Anything' (also
available on Amazon)

"Incredibly, Ross has now written a series of Children's
books about me (and Daisy). This is the first one!"

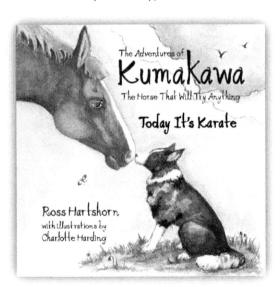

Printed in Great Britain
by Amazon

16754995R00108